Evolution to Equity

The Founder's Guide to People, Culture & Inclusion

Evolution to Equity

The Founder's Guide to People, Culture & Inclusion

By
Kalyn Romaine

This book is humbly dedicated to my grandma and namesake, Nancy Romain, who cultivated my potential from birth;

my Uncle Ronald, who pushed me as a founder before I saw it in myself;

the Northwestern Center for Talent Development, who taught me the art and science of book writing;

Willie Bell Gibson, who celebrated me as a writer and ignited my love of language;

and Professor Helen Fox, who modeled through her intellect and poise how to Unteach Racism.

Table of Contents

Introduction

Chances are you picked up this book for selfish reasons, and that's okay. You either want to beat the competition, make the world a better place for your children, or be recognized as a company where your employees and customers can be themselves. You want to learn everything you need to know in order to do the work, reach that peak, and say you have arrived. All of these reasons are selfish with good intentions – unfortunately, they are not realistic.

People are a mess, and that includes you. Being a founder requires a willingness to work through your messiness. You have been shaped by your upbringing, community beliefs, and socially-accepted judgments, which have influenced all of your decisions until now. Most importantly, that shaping influences how you build your company and its culture. This book will help you name your mess and take action to reverse its impact on you, your executive team, and your organization.

This is the heart of evolution. You will outgrow parts that no longer serve a purpose while growing new parts of yourself and your team that you need to thrive. The same messiness which helped you become a founder can be your undoing in the next phase of business. That's why I call this your guide to People*, culture, and inclusion (PCI). PCI includes a delightful experience for employees, candidates, vendors, the surrounding community, and customers (People); a rewarding and nurturing environment where those people can be true to themselves (culture); and a system of belonging that balances power, influence, and privilege (inclusion). Navigating the challenges of PCI is not easy, and it can be messy, but the results are worth it.

> *When the term "People" is capitalized throughout the book, I am referring to the functional area, commonly known as HR.*

9

It may comfort you to know I'm a mess too. My past includes anti-Blackness, homophobia, transphobia, and socioeconomic bias. I've discovered the roots of my discrimination stemmed from my upbringing as a Black Christian woman who attended "gifted" schools with other privileged children. I was raised in Detroit, Michigan in a predominantly Black, socially-homogeneous community. To say I had blind spots is an understatement. While studying at the University of Michigan in Ann Arbor, I suddenly found myself in a mostly white*, affluent community. This dichotomy was the beginning of my personal evolution to equity.

Years later, I made the choice to grow professionally. The field of diversity and inclusion, at that time, meant federal compliance and surface-impact projects like annual training sessions rather than true business transformation, so I never envisioned it becoming a career path for me. My initial reasons for prioritizing inclusion were not entirely altruistic. I was motivated by the desire to fit into privileged social circles at work and make more money. That selfish choice formally catalyzed my career and influenced what has become my work at Dream Forward Consulting.

People, culture, and inclusion (PCI) work combines business administration, sociology, economics, psychology, anthropology, and many other fields. In practice, you may recognize PCI as organizational development (OD), human resources (HR), and diversity, equity, and inclusion (DEI). It's a multi-layered discipline, which will stretch you beyond any of your previous academic studies. This is why it's so important to be a continuous learner and always take the position of curiosity and humility. You don't know what you don't know, and that is okay.

*Throughout this book, "white" will not be capitalized because it is not an actual race but a descriptor. If that's hard to deal with, accept that not everything that doesn't make sense to you needs to be changed for you.

10

Today, I am an advocate for marginalized groups, and I am still on my own evolution journey. I am uncovering then unlearning my biases every day as a founder, organizational psychologist, coach, and thought leader in People, culture, and inclusion. I now support leaders in PCI initiatives to help them do the same work I am doing. As much as this book is a manual for you to become a PCI leader in your own company, it's also the autobiography of my own evolution journey – the messiness and the mistakes that have led me to become a leader in this space. We have all made mistakes in the past. As you read my advice to you, just know that it stems from either my own blunders or those I've helped my clients work through. A lot of times, it's both.

My professional background includes sociology, psychology, management, and public policy, which are all disciplines that inform my multi-layered approach. Throughout this book, I am asking you to explore your own multi-layered approach as well. Your evolution journey includes these layers of yourself and what you have to unpack and unlearn. You are not alone. Again, I have had to do all of this too. Everyone has their own unique journey. Since we're all working through the messiness, we need others to point out where we can change. In this book, I'm that person.

I won't talk down to you. In fact, I use "we" throughout the book because we are in this together. I am not here to judge or preach; however, I'm sure you will experience discomfort at least once. Though the process is uncomfortable, it's necessary. I'm asking you to do away with some of your prior conditioning so you can be primed, ready, and able to understand the information I am offering. Be open-minded so you can shorten the learning curve to become a better founder and leader.

This book is written for founders of startup organizations and business leaders who have started a new company and lead a *small* team. It's better to start your evolution now when your company is new. Being a startup on an evolution journey means you get to begin a company's legacy the right way, instead of waiting and creating a disaster you will have to clean up later. It is the difference between turning a tugboat and the Titanic.

If you are a founder or leader reading this book, the three most important takeaways will be distillation, clarity, and self-discovery.

The first takeaway is distilling your intentions in this work and understanding your current position on the evolution journey. This means sifting through the possibilities, challenges, and hopes for how PCI will transform your company and team. The distillation process can be simultaneously thrilling and painful because it is primarily a confrontation of your "why," your targets, and your environment.

Second, you will clarify your company's position in PCI, specifically how others are going to see you and your work. The market and your consumers will have preconceived notions about you just because you exist, regardless of your intentions. When you ignore public opinions and current trends, you hurt your company's brand. You must be aware of the risks and past transgressions associated with your industry and the geographic locations where you perform work. Even if you had nothing to do with the actions causing those beliefs, it will be up to you to prove your company is different.

The third piece is self-discovery. As the founder of a startup, you may not have had a lot of executive coaching experience or a safe place to have these conversations. A lot of founders sit in bubbles, which creates tons of blind spots. As a founder, you are responsible for being aware of the impact you, your team, and your company have on the world around you. You don't get to just reap the benefits of being a pioneer and avoid being part of some potential problems. This is your work as a founder – to grow and change.

As a founder myself, I know you can feel overwhelmed by the journey at times. You have to create products, hire staff, manage the team, and generate revenue. You have more tasks than time and energy – I get it. You're also going to want to ask the people closest to you to validate who you are becoming. Because you are probably surrounded by at least a few folks who are very similar to you, that's not going to be helpful for you on your evolution journey. It's easier to support what has always been comfortable than challenge you.

This is internal and personal work that will eventually reflect outward. There are going to be moments of loneliness on this journey. Expect this. There will be moments when you have to fight against the people you thought you knew. Go ahead. Do it. There will be moments when you're going to want to stop this work altogether. Sometimes, it's okay to take a break and give yourself some grace. Just don't do it for too long and not when it really counts. This is a lifelong journey. I'm going to help you set the tone of the evolution journey for you, your team, and your organization.

PCI either reforms or performs, meaning you're either actively changing your company's story or you're simply entertaining yourself. I went from performing to reforming, starting with myself. My upbringing made me passionate about equity for the Black community, but I didn't realize I was just performing my advocacy for everybody else. Supporting one group to the detriment of others reinforces the fragility of bias; it's a charade and does not create systemic change. I now prioritize reformation by advocating for all marginalized groups to experience equity.

Before we dig in, be prepared. Anticipate what your mind might want to do with the information I'm going to give you. The natural instinct is to revert back to what you already know because it feels comfortable. The mind will want to reject this new information because it's too busy or overwhelmed. Push past this instinct.

One of the most significant areas of discomfort will be language. Semantics matter, so I will do my best to communicate both the meaning and tone of keywords in the PCI space. This means I may use a word in the literal sense, which runs counter to pop culture's tendency to bastardize language. This bastardization process is especially true for language common to marginalized groups. Other times, I may use words and phrases in fresh ways to expand your understanding of a concept. You will push your limits of human understanding, particularly around the way we use language in PCI. Language sometimes loses its salinity as it gains popularity. Instead of allowing the language to lose its flavor and become dry, this book will help you become energized by language and understand all of the various ways it can be applied to push and expand your understanding.

Because these concepts are so much more nuanced than we've been led to believe, you're going to hear the same words and concepts multiple times in this book. In that regard, I want you to treat it like a textbook, where the concepts build over time. Just like algebra, it builds on the basics of addition, subtraction, multiplication, and division, and then takes you from one level to the next level and the next. In the same way, you will see a basic definition and various applications of it. Then, you're going to start to see the correlations between those definitions. The correlations, progressions, and distinctions are all critical to evolution.

By the end of this book, you'll be clear on where you currently stand, who you need to become, and where your company needs to grow. But don't be fooled. Even though we are going to give you everything you need to make these things happen, the work is not easy. As founders, it is easy to task everyone around you with what *they* need to do while forgetting that everything starts with *you*. So, let's start with the most important person on this journey – YOU!

PCI for You

Inequity is experiential disparity or injustice, and it is not theoretical. It isn't just "four score and seven years ago" – it embodies lived experiences. If we continue to think of inequity as abstract, we will always "other" other people and absolve ourselves from taking any responsibility, which perpetuates systemic inequity. Because inequity is experiential disparity, or the lived experience of discrimination, the disparity deepens the more we live in the marginalized traits of our identity. The experience of inequity - as a person of privilege or one of marginalization - shapes how we view the world.

This first section is where you will gather the tools needed to understand yourself, your background, and how it has shaped your worldview. All journeys start somewhere, and your somewhere starts with you. Internal and intrapersonal change is more difficult than delegating change to and for others. Think of this as preparation for leading your company's PCI work. Learning, confronting, and transforming yourself will be a model for the journey you will lead your team and organization through. Your tenacity will set the stage for deep transformation in others.

Chapter 1: Dimensions of Identity

One of the loneliest parts of the evolution to equity is realizing the complexity of your own identity. We have been conditioned to seek likeness with others for survival, but we are all made up of more than 50 dimensions of identity. Some of these dimensions will change over time while others remain fairly static. You may go from being child-free to being a parent of four. This change in caregiver status will likely impact your identity in other areas of your life as well, such as socioeconomic status. On the other hand, while gender is typically considered an immovable dimension, the expansion of our collective understanding of gender identification makes the dimension more complex and fluid.

There is a push-pull mechanism of external factors determining how we assert our self-definition. External factors push us to use labels created by authority figures in society, regardless of how we may want to label ourselves. These factors also pull us into categories that can limit or distort how we see the human value in ourselves and others. This mechanism is commonly known as the cycle of socialization. The cycle of socialization is the sequence of predetermined categorizations and social roles we are conditioned to embody. Developed by Bobbie Harro, the framework illustrates how we learn to "be" in a world full of inequity and social hierarchies. It occurs cyclically and consistently, whether we are actively involved in its perpetuation or not.

The cycle of socialization begins before we are born. Ever heard of a gender reveal? It continues in our families and local communities. How did birth order impact your voice in the family, or how did your gender determine what activities were acceptable and which were not? The cycle gets reinforced through our educational and work experiences, with our friend groups and coworking relationships, and our neighborhoods and governments. All of these entities tell us who we are and reward us when we play our roles accordingly. A major part of our evolution journey is gaining clarity on all the layers of our identity, their interconnectivity, and their relationship to our worldview.

Recognizing those limitations and the push-pull mechanism of internal and external influences is fundamental to every evolution journey. So many of us categorize the journey as a matter of personal will, but our evolution is always contextualized in our social, political, and economic circles.

Understanding Identity As Layers

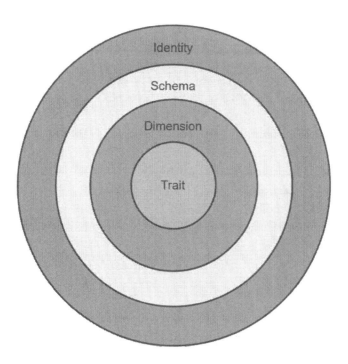

Identity is the combination of all of the traits we identify with in our various dimensions. While it may be common for people to share some traits of identity with each other, it's very rare that two people share the same identity. There are over 50 dimensions of identity (and counting).

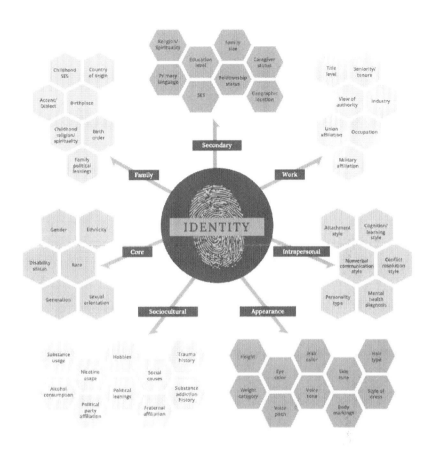

These dimensions are grouped by what I call schema, which is, by definition, a framework for categorizing and understanding information. The seven schemas group how we think about ourselves and place the world around us into categorical descriptors. The seven schemas used to classify identity are core, secondary, work, family, intrapersonal, sociocultural, and appearance.

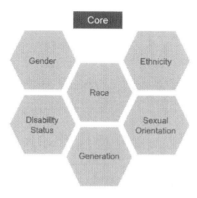

The core schema has a catalytic effect, which means its dimensional traits trigger the probability of what other traits will be. The core dimensions are gender, ethnicity, disability status, race, generation, and sexual orientation. As an example, if someone's gender is male, then they will likely not have other identity traits such as being a birth mom. On the other hand, they would be more likely to have more senior-level job titles and have a higher socioeconomic status. The inverse would be true if their gender was female. The core schema includes the dimensional traits of identity which are most likely to determine our "lot" in society.

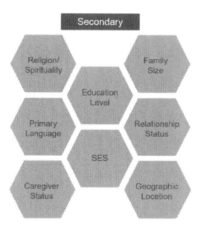

The secondary schema also determines many of the other dimensions. This schema determines how society chooses to limit your access to opportunities. The secondary dimensions are religion/spirituality, primary language, socioeconomic status, education level, relationship status, family size, caregiver status, and geographic location. If someone lives in the United States of America and their primary language is English, they may have access to better occupations in the U.S. because they speak the primary language of the country.

I call these two schemas core and secondary because they are the most commonly regarded aspects of our identity. Whether it's segmenting groups into voting blocks, categories for job applications, or creating clothing departments, these schemas rule the labeling process. They are most likely to impact access and quality of life. Ironically, the core and secondary schema may not be the most important to us as individuals; however, society places a premium on them as a determining factor of our lived experiences. Sorting out this difference between what's important to you versus society will further you in your evolution to equity.

Aside from the core and secondary schemas, there is also a work schema. Work is all about how we show up in our professional universe, including how we are titled, the affiliations defining our career paths, and how we develop our professional masks. These dimensions include title level, seniority/tenure, views of authority, industry, union affiliation, occupations, and military affiliation. It is important to realize how, in certain lines of work, we might tend to lean more heavily into our professional mask as our identity there. Take, for example, a union tradesperson, a member of a professional association like a doctor, or even a military veteran. There are certain characteristics people expect you to embody when you work in one of these fields and certain assumptions people make about your personality traits, both positive and negative. You may be deemed more reliable for having a military background or more intelligent because you are a doctor.

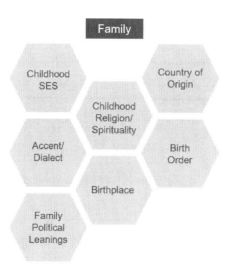

Then, the family schema includes the earliest and biologically closest set of identity dimensions because it shapes the earliest parts of our personality and external relationships. Dimensions of the family schema include birthplace, accent/dialect, birth order, childhood religion/spirituality, childhood socioeconomic status, country of origin, and familial political leanings. These characteristics tend to be the ones we are most likely to hold in confidence, particularly when our adult life is drastically different. If you were born into a family where a Southern drawl was common, you may become self-conscious about it and work to lessen it when put into situations with others from different backgrounds. The same could be said for someone who grew up poor and has now "made it," but doesn't want anyone else to know. In many ways, that may significantly impact how a founder shows up in PCI efforts because they'll make assumptions about what other people should be able to overcome or do as a result.

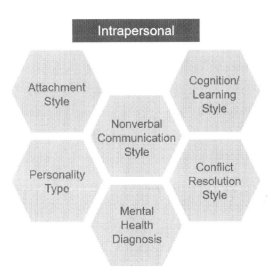

Unlike family dimensions, intrapersonal dimensions are like invisible drivers. These are not as easily named as some of the other dimensions. These happen internally, whether or not others have a chance to actually see and name them. Some of the dimensions in this schema are attachment style, cognition/learning style, nonverbal communication style, conflict resolution style, personality type, and mental health diagnosis. If someone never witnessed you in even the most minor conflict, they may never know what your style is until there is a blowup. Mental health diagnoses are another dimension in this schema. The sometimes subtle or unseen behaviors of mental illnesses make it easier to hide them. (It's important to note not all behavioral issues indicate a mental illness though, and no mental illness is an excuse to treat people inhumanely or unfairly.)

The sociocultural schema is the combination of social and cultural factors. They reflect how we express ourselves through group interactions. These dimensions rarely stand completely on their own. These include substance usage, alcohol consumption, nicotine usage, political party affiliation, hobbies, political leanings, social causes, fraternal affiliation, trauma history, and substance abuse history. Think about a working-class person of color battling addiction versus an affluent white person who does the same. The former is usually vilified in the public eye while the latter receives sympathy and support.

The sociocultural dimensions are frequently dependent on socioeconomic and caregiver statuses. There is research showing that as you age and achieve more wealth and status, the more likely you will be to lean conservative in political matters. So, even if you've always considered yourself a centrist, quite a few of your views may end up leaning more toward the right. It is the same way someone who has never had kids before might change some of their views on guns and school safety once they become a parent for the first time. Transparently, I have noticed several of my political views shift as I age and grow my wealth; I'm still processing the shift but have much more empathy for others experiencing the same transition.

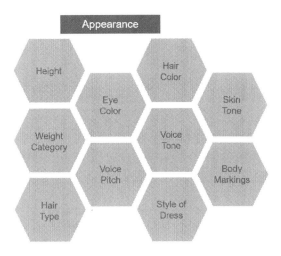

Lastly, the appearance schema focuses primarily on physical characteristics such as height, weight category, eye color, voice pitch, voice tone, hair color, skin tone, body markings, hair type, and style of dress. A combination of these factors produces an attraction or repellent due to societal norms. As I write this, my hair is blonde, and I am getting far more positive attention than I ever did when it was my natural black-brown tone. My hair has been an attraction magnet because people perceived me as braver and more sophisticated because I stepped outside of social expectations. If someone has dark skin, it is commonly assumed they should not have blonde hair. The same goes for height, weight, physical fitness, and so on. We prejudge how someone "should" look based on our own biases.

All of these schemas and dimensions, on their own, lack meaning and context. It's the intersection of the dimensions, especially across schemas, that starts to add meaning and influence outcomes. For a full list of the dimensions of identity, there is a chart provided at the end of this book. Read through the definitions and think about how their various combinations lead to judgments and assumptions.

Intersectionality

All of these dimensions create layers of complexities, and those layers are known as intersectionality. Intersectionality is a legal term coined by Kimberlé Crenshaw, a law professor and attorney, in the 1980s. The term was used to describe the double bias Black women experience as they navigate both racial and gender discrimination. It was inspired, in part, by a lawsuit against General Motors (GM) to prove a Black woman was denied a promotion due to systemic bias. The central argument posited that it couldn't be gender bias because white women were considered for promotion, and it couldn't be racial bias because Black men were considered as well. The plaintiff countered that the intersection of both gender and race creates a unique bias different from each individual bias.

I have expanded my own definition of intersectionality. My definition posits that layers of identity dimensions create a unique social experience, whether it be one of power, privilege, influence, or inequity. For example, a straight, white, cisgender, heterosexual male has all of those layers of dimensions to form an almost impenetrable force field, which a disabled, Asian, transgender woman will never experience. The first person's experience of power, privilege, and influence *creates* the second person's experience of inequity.

Intersectionality is the reason why people who have parts of their identity in a marginalized group can still be biased themselves. Having one marginalized dimension doesn't mean you can't also marginalize or show bias towards someone else. When I look back at my own life, intersectionality is the reason why I was homophobic as a Black woman. Although I sit in a marginalized dimension because of my race and gender, I also sit in a dimension of power and privilege as a cisgender, heterosexual person. This can feel confusing, but it's one of our most important "aha" moments in evolution. Founders must be comfortable with the complexity of intersectionality to understand how intersectionality creates disparate outcomes in PCI within our organizations.

Chapter 2: External Factors

External factors power the push-pull mechanism among our dimensions of identity like electrical currents. These factors determine our access to power, privilege, and influence, or our potential to experience inequity through cycles of socialization. Privilege is both a causal and an effectual element of power and influence. If I have privilege, it is easier for me to acquire power and influence; likewise, if I have power and influence, it's easier for me to be privileged in many scenarios. This push and pull of privilege might cause us to behave in certain kinds of ways we might not have otherwise chosen.

If I believe that, as the founder and CEO, I should be paid much higher than the lowest-paid employee in the company, I might be pushed into setting my compensation packages based on my beliefs related to the dimension of my job title. Conversely, the pull might be that I purposely avoid creating career growth pathways for my lower-level employees because I want to maintain the same level of income inequality.

Privilege

Privilege is the set of special concessions and entitlements we experience due to hegemony (one group's dominance over another). It is not only what we get to experience but what we have the opportunity to avoid experiencing. As a white man, you may have been conditioned to interact with law enforcement as a necessary protection mechanism in your neighborhood, but you also don't have to experience police brutality at the same rate a Black man does. Your archetypal characterization of police is based on your community's experience. While one person might experience the weight of the entire criminal justice system when they see an officer, another person might only see "the police."

Privilege is easy to acknowledge when viewed as an entitlement, like an extra freebie, but can be difficult to accept when viewed as an experience in absentia, like avoiding an experience or consequence that people from another group might routinely endure. For example, men are assumed to have inherent leadership capabilities and may have a natural advantage when interviewing for management roles because of their sex. Men also get to avoid rerouting their walk home or to the store in order to avoid catcalling. Privilege affords its beneficiaries naiveté on how harmful bias can be; they do not always see the negative effect it has on others.

It wasn't until the highly publicized murder of George Floyd in 2020 that people began to force a reckoning in police brutality towards people of color, not just with murders or savage beatings, but with traffic stops. Until then, few people really cared to collect national data about it, and even fewer would have published it even if it was collected. While this is not the first time in our country that we saw death at the hands of racial inequality on the national media level, it was one of the first times most of us were galvanized against the injustice. Think of that in comparison to the Rodney King beating in 1991 where we all saw the same footage, but many were divided on who to blame.

We don't like to acknowledge our privilege because we all like to believe we are the source of our own growth, development, and success. Especially in Western cultures, we have been socialized to think our individual effort has earned us the spots we occupy in our lives. This is particularly true for founders because everybody loves the bootstrap story. Just like it's much less marketable to tell people you got into Harvard as a legacy candidate because your father went there, it's equally less marketable to say you had the social capital available to network with people who could invest in your company and leverage that network to raise millions of dollars to grow it. That truth doesn't sound nearly as sexy as saying, "I was frustrated with the pace of my classes, so I dropped out of college, but I had a brilliant idea to change the world and am making it happen." Those bootstrap stories turn people on, and as a founder, we have to be aware of that privilege and acknowledge it.

Power vs. Influence

Power is a form of direct authority and control. In the workplace, we might see this play out in the relationships between a manager and the employees who directly report to them. Sure, there may be cultures where open dialogue and collaboration are encouraged, but a manager has the power to dictate the career path of those under them. Performance reviews, promotions, and terminations are all in their hands.

Influence is a much more covert method of control, and it ultimately starts and ends with the founder. Though you might be thinking the founder owns the company so power would be more appropriate, this is not always the case. Because of our position and prestige, we don't always need to *tell* people to do certain things. Our employees will model our thoughts, actions, and beliefs in order to gain favor or stay in the founder's good graces, regardless of our intent.

Hegemony

Hegemony is a sociological concept that explains the dominance of certain groups over others. It hinges on power, privilege, and influence and is fortified by inequity. Antonio Gramsci, a Marxist philosopher, defined cultural hegemony as the ways in which a ruling social class manipulates values and norms. This traditional definition from Gramsci is based on class warfare, but for the purposes of this book, we are considering hegemony to be any form of social or cultural dominance. I consider hegemony inevitable in group settings, especially since it can occur across any identity dimension.

We can identify hegemony by understanding the power and privilege centers in a group. When hegemony is working well, individuals don't have to actively employ it; it goes on autopilot to control groups. It is established through shared language and bureaucracy, which, in sociological terms, is the system of economic, political, and social control in our daily life. This can be as small as requiring a password to access company systems or as large as requiring five approvers for business purchases over $10,000.

Hegemony can be established in a company by saying our staff should be referred to as team members instead of employees. Disney calls their theme park employees cast members. Although those people aren't cast members when they go home, something about the Disney work environment makes them immediately shift their self-perception and identity to define themselves as cast members. When used in a positive and uplifting way like this, hegemony can bring a team together and rally them behind the mission at hand, but the opposite can hold true if we are not careful.

One of my clients was experiencing an issue within their executive team because of this intersection of power, influence, and hegemony – and it's not what you think. Although the entire group shares the same race, sexual orientation, and generation, the executive team is gender-diverse. So, where is the issue? Industry. All but one of these executives worked at the same company prior to transitioning to this company. Hegemony festered through their shared professional background, and they clung to its resulting power and influence. The executive who did not work at the same company, while equally qualified and dedicated to the new organization, was not treated the same way because of their industry dimension. This ultimately resulted in their exit from the company, which could have been avoided if the founder was paying attention to the uncomfortable work environment.

Identity Expression

We act out hegemony through identity expression patterns. Identity expression is how we convey the dimensional traits of our identity; we do that through dimension prominence, dominance, and comfort.

- Dimension prominence is typically performed through dimensions that are conspicuous, such as looks and other easily labeled attributes, such as race or gender. For example, we may make assumptions about someone's socioeconomic status based on the clothes they wear or the color of their skin. Dimension prominence fills the need to compartmentalize others and resolve inner conflict.
- Dimension dominance could be conspicuous, but It Is typically based on dimensional traits of identity previously affirmed or rewarded. It fills our need to feel validated or appear strong and valued. For example, if I use my "white person voice" when I take care of business or handle administrative matters in my life, it's because my past experiences have confirmed that people are more likely to want to work with me when I speak this way. If I got the job I wanted when I used a shortened version of my name, I'm going to continue to use that name because it delivered my desired outcome.
- Dimension comfort could be conspicuous, but it is based on ease of expression or for internal affirmation. It fills the need to validate our inner child or calm our emotional triggers. If I slip into a Jamaican accent when I get angry, that's an example of identity comfort if I'm not normally using that accent. Another great example is the use of AAVE (African American Vernacular English) and code-switching when in a group with other Black people.

I'm at a point in my life where I don't usually code-switch to pacify others; instead, I simply choose not to say certain words or phrases if I'm not in predominantly Black spaces. For me, it's more of a reflexive gatekeeping than an intentional switch for acceptance. I use certain language to create a sense of belonging with other Black people who may be more comfortable with that particular style of speech. It signals my sense of belonging with them while subtly signaling to others that this is not a dimensional trait I share with them.

We have all expressed dimension prominence, dominance, and comfort. It's not something one group experiences more than another. It shows up in religion, race, political preferences, military affiliation, appearance, and any other dimension. All three expressions are always at play. For some people, navigating between the three can create a sense of false identity. Kenji Yoshino describes this phenomenon as covering. Covering can feel like being forced to live a life someone else has imposed on us, restricting the ability to ever be our authentic self. This inner conflict can be eased or inflamed by the organizational cultures we create as founders.

Chapter 3: Family, Education, and Community

Family, education, and community are three external factors that affect our identity expression and, therefore, impact our evolution to equity. Your family is your first PCI teacher because they determine many of the traits within the dimensions of your identity. They're the first indicator of your place in marginalization hierarchies, or the system of ranking biases. Even more important, your family can either be your evolution journey's champion or blocker. For example, if you are the child of a white, affluent, gay couple, you may grow up with an inclusion lens that leans toward LGBTQ+ inclusion. Your lens may simultaneously have a blind spot for the experiences of racial injustice or socioeconomic bias.

Family

Our family's influence on our evolution is not always explicit. They teach us what to appreciate or despise through modeling, punishment, or reward, which sets our expectations for other connections and relationships. These expectations impact how we expect others to speak to us, interpret our speech, and treat us. Family is also our first experience with safety or lack thereof. We learn early on what behaviors, thought patterns, and language are considered safe for us. Those experiences of constant emotional danger or safety will lead us to despise people who threaten our safety as adults.

Some of the dimensions of identity which are particularly important in family are birth order, gender, race, ethnicity, personality type, attachment style, nonverbal communication style, and appearance. If most of your family members are quiet, intellectual types but you are more boisterous and artistic, your family's rejection or constant attempts to correct what they perceive as "bad" behavior will teach you early on that conforming to other people is necessary to your survival. This could lead to a subconscious loathing of expressive colleagues who refuse to conform to dress or speech norms at work.

Education

Education is another precarious element of our evolution. The dimensions of identity most impacted by school are socioeconomic status, gender, race, disability, learning style, appearance, and religion. We learn early what it takes to be accepted in a multidimensional ecosystem. Families typically operate with clear power dynamics, but school is different because you have the power and influence dynamic of peers and adults. In families, there is usually an authority figure, such as a parent, who controls your peers, who are usually your siblings. On the other hand, teachers and other educators may not have the same level of capability or interest to be an authority figure. While a teacher may have thirty students in her classroom, a parent likely only has a few children who they have influence over. Furthermore, the peer-adult conflict may exist in both school and our home with different motivators; we aren't graded for our obedience at home like we are in the classroom.

School has a conflicting power and influence dynamic, which teaches us early about competing interests. If you are considered gifted in a low-income school with no capacity to support your intellectual curiosity, you might face bullying from your peers but be deified by the teacher for your intellect. That creates a push-and-pull conflict of interest between keeping yourself in the teacher's good graces and avoiding the bullying of your peers, which doesn't go away as you grow up. Instead, it shows up in different ways as an adult, and one of the most common ways is through people-pleasing. As a founder, if we are afraid of being laughed at or bullied by others in our peer group, we'll avoid taking bold risks in PCI initiatives despite our employees asking for us to show up differently on their behalf.

It is important to note the experience one has in school varies greatly based on socioeconomic status. When you are in a lower socioeconomic bracket, the focus leans toward following directions rather than becoming a critical thinker. You are more likely to be measured by the ability to perform rote tasks like memorization or worksheet completion, which are meant to be filled in exactly as prescribed. If you want to move prior to the end of a period, you need permission from a teacher or authority figure. Discipline and obedience are the themes of the lower socioeconomic classes. My earliest childhood educational experiences fell into this category.

When you move into middle-class education, which represents most of my childhood educational experience, the focus is on following the "right way to do it." You have some level of freedom or flexibility, but there is still a prescribed method for getting stuff done. This is due to the middle class's fragility. At this level, you are not poor enough to qualify for most types of assistance, but at the same time, you could always be one paycheck or one generation away from poverty. Doing things "right" gives a false sense of security and hope. Many urban magnet and charter schools fall into this category.

In upper-class education, the focus is on creating new and/or managing existing systems. Examples of these types of schools would be private schools, boarding schools, or elite religious schools, just to name a few examples. The environment offers more choices, more creativity, and more opportunities because the education system encourages them to build and rule the world around them. I experienced this during undergrad at Michigan.

There will always be exceptions to these class differences, but my own educational journey affirms this path. I started kindergarten at a neighborhood school where we simply completed worksheets daily. I was considered gifted and skipped grades quickly before my teacher and principal lobbied to transfer me to a magnet elementary school, which I attended through middle school and matriculated to a magnet high school. The magnet schools were firm middle-class institutions. We had access to advanced placement (AP) courses, the arts, college tours, and the prestige of being named as the best schools in Detroit's public school system. But, we also faced the pressure of conforming to narrow views of Black respectability politics and prescribed success paths.

Ivy League schools, elite state schools like the University of Michigan and Michigan State University, and prominent HBCUs like Howard University and Spelman College would visit on-site to recruit us. I remember when representatives from Brown University told us they didn't use a traditional grading system. Performance was instead measured by our ability to create a meaningful body of work. I couldn't comprehend that level of freedom until I studied at the University of Michigan. I struggled my first semester because my professors and graduate assistants were adamant I could write papers using any argument as long as I followed a prescribed format for the paper itself like page limits and citation style. I panicked. Years later, I felt a little sad for the younger version of myself who had such counter-cultural views but lacked the self-confidence to express them freely through my work.

To be clear, the caste system of education has been designed to keep existing economic groups stagnant. I do not fault or demonize any of my professors, teachers, or administrators for their conditioning. I recognize they were simply preparing me for the next phase they could fathom based on their own worldview. They honestly believed their actions were keeping me safe, but that safety reinforces invisible boxes of bias and inferiority.

This constant pressure to fit into the educational system's prescribed outcomes can feel unbearable for teenagers, especially as they begin to discover their identities. They may realize they prefer to date people outside of their race or have romantic feelings toward someone of the same gender. They may be diagnosed with ADHD, which makes them realize they learn differently than others and need support. It's also possible the diagnosis is incorrect because it was based on social norms and certain nonconforming behaviors. Like teenagers, founders change too, and we change as the people around us change. We have to learn to navigate all of that in an ever-evolving landscape.

Community

Outside of our families and school, we are part of a larger community when we grow up. We often don't even have the full scope of our community at first, but we learn it over time and in pieces. Our community consists of all of these people from our parents' friends and coworkers, to the bodega owner, to the neighborhood patrol officer. We come to see our community almost as if rubbing grime off our glasses. When we look through the lenses, we might see something fuzzy or the picture looks a little weird, but as we start wiping the glass and keep wiping, it becomes more clear. That wiping process has an effect on us as we grow up.

You probably didn't grow up knowing you had a race until someone in your community told you. That person could have been a family member, a teacher, a classmate, or a random person from your neighborhood. You also didn't know there were particular responsibilities or expectations of your gender until someone in your community told you. Maybe someone at your house of worship told you to start sitting with your legs crossed because that's more ladylike. We are constantly getting cues of what we can and cannot do and what is considered appropriate. These cues form our early mental maps. The community is our first experience with the benefits and pitfalls of either homogeneity or diversity.

This is where a lot of my personal evolution journey transformed. I grew up in a predominantly Black community in Detroit, but because I went to magnet schools, I had experiences with mixed-income families. I went to school with some of the wealthier kids in Detroit, working-class kids like myself, and middle-income kids from all over the city. It was a mixed bag of kids because Detroit, as a whole, is a pretty unique city. My experience with racial homogeneity but socioeconomic diversity gave me a very particular lens through which I see PCI possibilities. I know what can happen when you give people access to the resources to grow. Unfortunately, I am also aware of some of the pitfalls of homogeneity and its resulting blind spots. I often forgot or failed to prioritize the needs of others who were different from me.

All three of these factors – family, school, and community – model what is acceptable or unacceptable. People don't always have to explicitly say what to do and what not to do; instead, we learn by watching the consequences or the rewards other people receive. These patterns are incredibly difficult to break once they're set, which is typically around the age of seven but definitely by the time you become a teenager.

As a founder, we get to choose how to treat the people who work for us when they need extra support and empathy to integrate into the company we're building. Remember that we could be asking them to fight against deeply ingrained beliefs and norms that have helped them survive up to this point. That's not to say we'll have a separate set of standards for everyone in the organization, but we can offer reasonable supports to help them flourish. Employees are not going to feel comfortable sharing their challenges in a business run like a dictatorship. We need to understand how the founder establishes power and influence norms to accommodate the team's needs. This way, they can operate as the best version of themselves and make meaningful contributions. When we operate more like a representative democracy, people trust us and want to do their best.

Chapter 4: Emocognition

A major key to understanding PCI is recognizing we have emotional connections to the stories we've been told about ourselves, others, and our place in the world. We also navigate the world through our thoughts. Our thoughts and feelings are interdependent. This connection is called emocognition.

Emocognition, a term I coined, is a hybrid of emotion and cognition. Emocognition combines two foundational human psychological processes and it is what drives our ability to navigate through the people, mental maps, and strategies influencing our evolution to equity. It drives our evolution by being our filter for understanding interpersonal relationships, reinforces the beliefs and memories driving our decisions, and helps or hinders us from taking meaningful action toward equity in our realm of influence. Emocognition is why someone might advocate for autistic children who remind us of our siblings but balk at the idea of reparations for African Americans who we feel should pull themselves up by the bootstraps like our immigrant ancestors. To help you understand emocognition as a hybrid phenomenon, I'll first explain emotion and cognition separately.

Emotion

Emotion is a three-step sequential process:
1. **Subjective experiences:** External stimuli which generates personal significance.
2. **Physiological responses:** Our bodies' reaction to a subjective experience.
3. **Behavioral responses:** External expressions of our feelings.

We classify emotion as a sequential process because our experiences drive our responses, and even those responses can build on each other. Let's say your subjective experience is poor customer service when a barista hands you the wrong coffee. You may not even be aware of your body's physiological response when your cheeks flush red with anger. You do, however, recognize when you yell at the barista.

Cognition

Cognition is the conscious and unconscious state of knowing. Unlike emotion, any of cognition's seven primary functions can happen without a particular sequence:

- **Knowledge acquisition:** A mental process where you obtain information, then assign and contextualize it with both meaning and significance based on the environment.
- **Learning:** The process of synthesizing information into knowledge.
- **Thought:** A process that influences decision-making, analytical reasoning, and problem-solving.
- **Attention:** Our ability to focus on an environmental stimulus.
- **Memory:** The capturing and archival of short-term and long-term events and their impact.
- **Perception:** An experiential process where our senses interpret stimuli to compel us to respond to the external environment.
- **Language:** A process where we use written and spoken words to communicate with ourselves and the world around us.

Facets of Emocognition

Emocognition is a complex relationship between mental and emotional processes which impact our ability to thrive through social change. Sometimes our emotions lead, and sometimes our cognition leads. In the latter, when a barista gets our coffee order wrong, the emotion of anger could have been triggered by the cognitive recollection of a past misstep in the same location. In the former, this emotion of anger could lead you to use the cognitive function of language to swear at the barista.

Emocognition includes four facets: risk, reward, values, and motivation. These facets intertwine and often depend on one another. For example, we measure our risk tolerance based on our values, and we are motivated by potential rewards to take or avoid action.

Risk

Risk, by definition, means potential exposure to disappointment. Risk tolerance falls on a spectrum ranging from aversion to embracement. Managing risk in our evolution to equity implies a willingness to manage potential disappointment with ourselves or others. It can also mean disappointment with the narrative we have been fed and the narrative we are hoping will emerge. This can show up as avoiding interracial friendships because of a memory of being warned to avoid them by our grandparents. The potential disappointment of family ostracism could lead to avoidance.

Reward

Reward is the validation of our choices. Rewards can be tangible or intangible and can come from internal or external sources. If you have a mandatory, morning-long, anti-sexual harassment training and you give them the afternoon off for completing it, the reward of time off gives them a mental break and joy at having free time. Rewards can also be detrimental or create dependencies, which undermine our evolution. If you're a founder who rewards "achieving results by any means," you may be inadvertently encouraging bullying or burnout as your team tries to meet your expectations to reap your rewards.

Values

Values are our egos' north star and grounding force. Values are relatively stable throughout our lives and help us to decode subjective experiences and make decisions. Values help us navigate executive functioning, a set of mental skills that help us to manage our lives. These functions are important for everyone in daily life but become increasingly more so with the amount of responsibility on our plate as a founder.

Ego comes from Freud's definition of the Self, which consists of three parts: the id, super id, and ego. The id is our reptilian brain or instincts, the super id is where we are bombarded with external and societal influences and messages, and our ego is focused on maximizing pleasure and minimizing pain. Our ego controls our values because it signals to our brains how to evaluate and respond to subjective experiences. For example, one of my top values is resilience because I grew up in poverty. When I encounter a challenge, my ego demands I find a solution instead of quitting. While this may seem noble, it also leaves me prone to overworking and burnout.

It is our responsibility as individuals to have clarity of Self and who we are. With so much external pressure, particularly around changing, this can be an area of PCI where founders get tripped up. To become an inclusive and more equitable founder, understanding our personal "why" and evolution goals helps us avoid being tossed around. We see what is real, substantial change and what might just be trendy.

Motivation

Motivation is slightly more complex than the other facets and consists of four qualities:
- **Money:** Capital and investment resources, which include cash, stock, equity, and organizational decision-making power.
- **Prestige:** The reputation and clout built through real or perceived accomplishments, which includes awards, publicity, and notoriety.
- **Safety:** Psychological and physical security, which includes job stability, trust, autonomy, and predictability.

- **Self-actualization:** The fulfillment of potential, which includes legacy, community building, self-advocacy, and purpose.

All four of these qualities combine to create a unique ratio, which is continually evolving and changing based on where someone is in their life or career. Emotions are frequent motivators for the shift in these ratios. Consider how a potential bonus can motivate us to work longer hours. The hope of extra money to pay off a credit card makes the work doable.

Emocognition in Evolution

Emocognition is an important compass on our evolution to equity. It is our reference point to understanding what triggers us, so we can discover the root of the trigger - the who, what, and why. It is a calibration tool for deciding how to plan our evolution. Do we focus on religious tolerance or eliminating ableism? Antiracism or closing the gender-based pay gap? Our emocognitive lens will tell us where we feel more comfortable taking action first. Lastly, it is our path to recognizing our True North. We may fool ourselves into believing we are much more culturally competent, committed to inclusion, and empathetic than we actually are. Emocognition snitches on us every time. If we cave into our biases when angry, face the chance to make life-changing money, or feed our need to take big risks, then we can't pretend to be mature in our evolution – just like we can't make True North south, no matter how many times we change directions.

Chapter 5: Elements of Evolution

I have described the evolution to equity as a journey because it will have many twists and forks. While those twists and forks will differ from person to person, there are three elements we will all have to manage: people, mental maps, and strategy. Each of these elements can be helpful or harmful, so as founders, we must be careful to assess and recalibrate often.

People

The people included in our evolution journey are both ourselves and others within three loci of influence. Think of these loci like a bullseye, and you are at the center of the bullseye. The first locus is our family and close friends. The second locus is our casual acquaintances and close colleagues, and the third is strangers and any new acquaintances. You transition through these three loci by varying levels of intimacy, length of engagement, and privilege. When attempting to inspire others to change, it is easier to influence the loci closest to us.

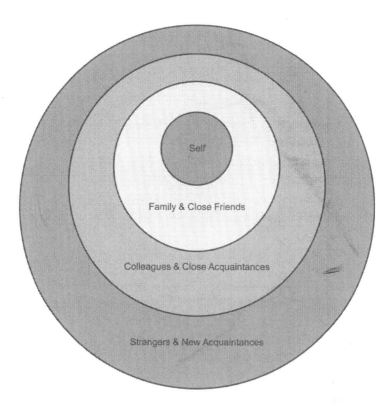

Intimacy

Intimacy involves physical, emotional, intellectual, and/or spiritual closeness. We typically build intimacy through shared or complementary identity traits; for example, we may feel more understood by others in our same age group. In a business setting, the more points of intimacy we have with the team, the easier it will be to get them to buy into the change we want to see enacted.

Length of Engagement

Length of engagement is about the amount of time we've known someone and the frequency and consistency of our interactions. The longer we know someone, the more opportunities we have to influence them, especially if we interact with them consistently. One example is how office cliques develop since they share a long history and many memories together. A new employee may struggle to fit into the circle because they do not share those memories or history.

Privilege

Privilege is both the entitlements and concessions we experience because of a relationship. As a founder, I have a lot of entitlements including permissions to delegate tasks and conversations to lead. I also have concessions such as access to discretionary spending. My teammates lack these privileges and subsequently have a much more limited experience in the company.

Mental Maps

A mental map is a subjective perception of the objective world. In other words, we interpret what we sense by what we subconsciously know and believe. This is where emocognition is really important because we can interpret what should be objective information through our subjective lens in an effort to avoid the cognitive dissonance of change. Mental maps reflect our biases and have four parts: sensory experience, emotional trigger, cognitive activation, and outward action.

Have a Sensory Experience

A sensory experience is simply an experience where we see, hear, smell, taste, or feel something. As another part of the sensory experience, our mental maps also determine whether or not we are in an environment safe enough to acquire and process new information.

Triggers Emotion

The sensory experience triggers your body and your mind in ways largely dependent upon your id, or instincts. This is where that emotional process activates, and what kicks off the process we discussed in Chapter 4. We often lean back into the deeply rooted mental processes and mental maps from early childhood if we are not careful to create new mental maps.

Activates Further Cognitive Processes

The triggers are far from where the mental map formation process ends and are inextricably linked to the seven cognitive processes we mentioned in Chapter 4. We call them triggers for a reason, because they spark involuntary responses such as memory recall and knowledge acquisition. Much of this happens subconsciously and can lead to hasty reactions or a complete shutdown.

Act Accordingly

Once we are aware of how certain words, phrases, or situations can impact those on the team, it is up to us to act accordingly going forward. This is a work in progress, but we should show visible improvement in the moments where it counts the most.

The collective outrage at George Floyd's murder relates to the creation of micro and macro mental maps. It might have slipped under the radar, like so many other instances if it hadn't happened during the early days of the COVID-19 pandemic. The majority of us were already on edge and experiencing sensory overload due to the ambiguity of the virus and unprecedented shelter-in-place restrictions. If those two things didn't happen at the same time, we might not have seen as much urgency around PCI, and this book might not have been written. Sensory overload contributed to the development of new mental maps.

This was not just a routine case of police brutality. The chaos pushed everyone to be at least a little more open to change. We wanted to change the whole system. But as soon as a couple of those catastrophic events subsided, so did our triggers. We leaned back into our old mental processes because the absence or distance from triggers can make us forget about change.

The collective permission to experience an emotional trigger is what made this instance different, and something we can put into perspective within your organization. Typically, founders need significant, catastrophic issues to make us even think about changing the way we currently do things. George Floyd's murder made conversations around inequity unignorable. Plus, the emotions of confusion, anger, and disbelief were so common it would be hard for any good leader to ignore them.

The world opened itself to the idea of change. How could we build an antiracist society? A workplace where racial bias didn't permeate every part of the system? These questions drove PCI practitioners like me to suggest and teach the behaviors which could make this a reality.

Language

The final aspect I want to mention, as it concerns mental maps, is language. How we are able to develop and become comfortable with appropriate language to describe PCI-related phenomena makes a huge difference in whether or not we stagnate or stay evergreen on our evolution journey. If you still refer to Black people as "colored folks" or "negros," your inability to move through modern language is going to stop you from being able to learn and grow. Language matters because it impacts how people perceive our maturity.

Strategy

Strategy is a startup's Achilles' heel. Most of your early strategy revolves around product development and getting to market. The second move will probably be around marketing and distribution. Almost all of your time and attention will be focused on making money and gaining visibility for your product or service. While revenue-generating activities are crucial for businesses at all stages, People and culture often take a backseat at this stage. Though we shouldn't ignore revenue in the quest to build a perfect culture, we do need to be conscious of balancing the two to ensure teammates who are with us at the beginning want to stick around to the next level.

The formal definition of strategy is a plan of action or policy designed to achieve a major goal. The key word in this definition is "plan" because it implies a definite finish and an assumption that change is necessary. Great strategy is a combination of reinforcing behaviors, leveraging mental maps, and connecting people. These three parts often undermine the way most companies approach PCI work because their strategy is reactionary. It's poorly thought-out, and it's not always clear what the specific added value will be to both the company and the communities impacted by the strategy. Many companies catalyze building PCI strategy through benchmarking, but that method is inherently flawed. The last five years have shown us that few, if any, companies are doing PCI well, so you will always be benchmarking against an imperfect ruler.

Strategy should be meaningful to you personally, as the founder, but also to the company's mission and vision. Great strategies are iterative. Even if it's just used to solve one problem, it should be scalable so we can continue to build on the excitement or success of what we achieved. Bad strategies stop at one problem. There are four elements of a great PCI strategy: a goal, relevant milestones, the stakeholders, and dependencies; and each one has its own threats and opportunities.

Goal

Many companies wait for a crisis to happen, then work on PCI for a bit until they feel like the crisis has passed. That's not effective. PCI goals should address the four motivations and stretch the organization. A good format for setting goals is to use the SMART goals layout: specific, measurable, action-oriented, relevant, and timed. All five of these have to be present for the goal to be meaningful.

Relevant Milestones

Milestones enable you to note progress along the way to achieving goals. Nobody is expecting the company to change the world in six months, but it's easy to become demotivated with longer goals. Since startups tend to be incredibly agile and shortsighted, the majority of their goals are set at 12 months or less, but PCI work usually takes a lot longer than 12 months to see meaningful progress.

Milestones help to manage distractions, demotivation, and scope creep. Scope creep can be called "mission creep" or "vision creep" as well, but it's the idea of internal or external factors that may slowly pull you off track from your goal. It's dangerous because we typically don't notice it happening until it's too late.

Stakeholders

It is a founder's responsibility to make sure every PCI goal and project is appropriately staffed and re-align people as necessary to achieve these goals. This requires an incredible amount of bravery, mental clarity, agility, and decisiveness. It's the founder's responsibility to recognize if someone on the team does not fit the role required for an organization to achieve their PCI goals.

A lot of founders shy away from this because they're depending on people who lack the competency and, in some cases, interest to do the work. We often lack the competency to be an executive leader of PCI and wind up taking on anyone who is willing to step up. However, that actually communicates to the team and customers from marginalized groups that they don't deserve the same level of care and competence as other business priorities, which is a bad look for the company.

Dependencies

Dependencies are steps that need to occur before completing another step in a project. PCI is one area where companies are notorious for missing dependencies. One of the most significant dependencies in PCI is data; in other words, do you have the right information, in time, to make good decisions? How often do we conduct surveys, focus groups, thorough exit interviews, and informal feedback from the team and customers? How often do we listen to the feedback and make changes?

All of the pieces of strategy are connected because understanding the gaps between knowledge, setting goals, and understanding risks and rewards all fit together. We can't appropriately set a goal if we lack knowledge. We can't do a proper risk assessment unless we have a meaningful goal and the right language to express it. Otherwise, we can't determine whether or not something is too risky.

We make decisions across the identity dimensions based on our own biases, and this is why strategy matters. It helps us avoid being underprepared and to stay motivated. The evolution journey, and its PCI work, means we involve the right people and understand how they influence us. It means we recognize how our mental maps influence how we create meaningful strategies that set, and keep, us in motion. Without motion, we're guaranteed to not do any good for anyone.

Chapter 6: Pause & Reflect

You've been through a lot in the last five chapters. You've begun to understand the ways in which your life experience and identity differ greatly from others in ways that can be harmful. You have unpacked how your brain and heart help or hinder the evolution to equity. And, you have started the difficult practice of delineating between all of the forces on that journey. That's a lot. You may even feel overwhelmed due to the overuse of your executive functions.

Executive functions and defense mechanisms are the brain's natural yet highly complex cognitive functions. There is a good chance you have probably worked yourself into a frenzy as you have tried to adopt this new information. Your defense mechanisms might be activated and overloaded because your brain has probably wanted to reject at least some of this information.

Executive functions and defense mechanisms relate to PCI because they are tied to our egos. In Chapter 4, we discussed the role of ego and PCI, specifically as your ego being a rationalizing mediator. It's how you navigate between your instinctive reactions (your id), and external components or pressures (the super id). The ego is right in the middle. Our executive functions and defense mechanisms can hurt us by pushing us to make decisions that could undermine our evolution journey. Though you cannot get away from executive functions or defense mechanisms, the goal is to be able to manage them in a way that takes you deeper into your evolution journey instead of holding you back.

Managing executive functioning and defense mechanisms requires an understanding of the cycle of socialization, motivations, mental maps, and the people around us. This is incredibly difficult work. This chapter is designed to acknowledge how tough it is to confront everything you thought you knew about yourself and the people around you. There are several executive functions and defense mechanisms at play in the evolution journey.

7 Types of Executive Functions

- **Self-awareness:** Self-directed reflection or action.
- **Inhibition:** One's ability to restrain oneself.
- **Nonverbal working memory:** The capacity to leverage expectation and memory to navigate time and space.
- **Verbal working memory:** The capacity to use language to retain short-term information.
- **Emotional regulation:** The ability to control emotions when experiencing external and internal triggers.
- **Motivation regulation:** The ability to navigate external and internal triggers to maintain or shift stimulation.
- **Problem-solving:** The capacity to develop and modify plans to achieve goals.

The definitions above are not meant to be all-encompassing and can vary based on the different applications within a specific organization and how they work with one another. Self-awareness and inhibition often go hand in hand because if you are not emotionally intelligent toward yourself (knowing your own proclivities and triggers), it will be almost impossible to manage your inhibition. At the leadership level, inhibition is not optional. I'm sure we all can think of leaders who have just completely failed their company and themselves because they had little self-control.

Nonverbal working memory and verbal working memory also play into this work because memory, as a function of cognition, will lead us to either ignore our triggers or put ourselves in a position where we mismanage our triggers because we refuse to acknowledge certain painful memories. This could be the memory of being humiliated as a kid and vowing to yourself to never be bullied again, which can cause you to operate from an emotionless state as a leader. Memories of being neglected as a child may lead you to be money-driven, so you can pay for companionship to satisfy your need for relationships. You may close off and be conflict-averse, causing you to refuse to address elephants in the room, which affects the company's and your own evolution journey.

Defense Mechanisms

Defense mechanisms are on the other side of executive functions. As much as executive functions are our delivery and integration of the best practices for self-management, our defense mechanisms are constantly driving the id to work. There are nine defense mechanisms, but the ones particularly related to PCI are repression, regression, sublimation, reaction formation, and projection. These mechanisms are how we instinctively protect our minds from what seems like an attack. We all use defense mechanisms in our personal and professional lives and likely know people who come to mind when we think about each of them. They are:

- **Repression:** Unconsciously suppressing negative thoughts.
- **Regression:** Coping with stress by behaving immaturely or inappropriately.
- **Sublimation:** Substituting an unacceptable behavior for another more socially-acceptable behavior.
- **Reaction Formation:** Replacing an unwanted behavior with an opposite and flamboyant behavior.
- **Projection:** Attributing our own negative thoughts or behaviors to others.

Executive functioning and defense mechanisms are constantly happening with each other. It's never an either-or. This is why it's such a complex function. As you work through your "aha" moments from this section, take a deep breath and acknowledge your own bravery for taking this first step. We have a way to go; however, you're confronting yourself before requiring more from others. That's a great start!

PCI for Your Executive Team

Understanding ourselves is only the first step in the founder's evolution to equity. The next step is understanding those closest to us, how they influence us, and the way their work intersects with our own. The executive team, or C-suite, is the closest in job title and company function to a founder. A high-functioning executive team can foster an equitable organization. When your executive team recognizes they are changemakers, approaches their work through an equity lens, and balances ownership of their own authenticity with flexibility, you set the organization up for success in People, culture, and inclusion (PCI). High functioning means embodying a number of qualities we see most clearly during conflict, crisis, or change. Some of these qualities are resilience, integrity, humility, empathy, and diplomacy. Even if we have all of these qualities listed, there is still work to do because functioning at a high level requires continuous improvements and adjustments.

The executive team is composed of the top leaders of the company. The founder is their supervisor, coach, and mentor. Founders are responsible for watching out for pitfalls and weaknesses among the executive team, as well as amplifying their strengths and assessing opportunities for growth. Founders often hire friends to the executive team or industry leaders they admire or deify, which is one of the costliest mistakes in both financial and cultural impact. We hire people who we like, trust, and believe will make the startup process less stressful, rather than intentionally designing a team that will work best for the company and not just our egos.

Chapter 7: Executive Team Purpose

It's nearly impossible to run a company alone, and running a company with a dysfunctional executive team is setting yourself up for failure. All teams serve three main purposes: to distribute labor, ensure quality, and accelerate progress. Distributed labor implies people having specialties, which suit their skills and interests. Ensuring quality is recognizing multiple perspectives in order to address every side of the work and then committing to excellence. Lastly, we progress quicker with more minds involved; additional people shave time off the growth process. This is especially true on the evolution journey. If even one aspect is missing, this stunts the entire company's PCI progress.

Teams should move with purpose, recognizing their collective importance and the gravity of each individual role. The purpose of the C-suite is to boost the four V's: vision, values, viscosity, and verticals.

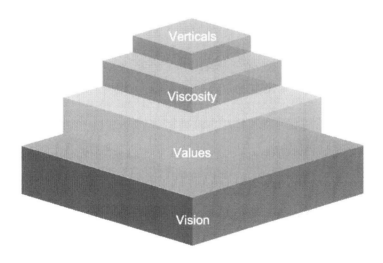

Vision

Vision should be every founder's highest priority. A vision is the company's ideal identity, meaning how it shows up in the world. If our vision is not improving the world in some way, what's the point of doing it? This leans on the idea that the vision should be inspirational and valuable. Each executive team member plays a role in defining and embodying the vision.

A founder's vision is usually to make a ton of money, change the world, go public, or sell. While admirable, the vision should extend to other goals like an equitable employee and candidate experience, fiscal responsibility, and smart growth to avoid unnecessary attrition and product sunsets. The latter set of goals is less sexy but is often more important.

A meaningful vision will:
- Signal behavioral standards. Vision is a preventative measure as much as a prescriptive one. It lets employees know how they should behave to fulfill the vision.
- Reflect the company's products and services. A tech company's vision is not going to be the same as a fast-fashion manufacturing company because they are providing two completely different products. A relatable vision keeps the company motivated.
- Influence more than just money. It creates a skeleton of the company's social and political identity too.

The scale of the company's vision matters too. If it's too big, it feels unattainable; if it's too small, it's boring to employees and customers. Think of cryptocurrency startups who have touted their ability to "completely upend the financial sector." They did just that as they crashed, disproportionately devastating Black investors in the process. A more reasonable vision would have allowed them to monitor their impact on marginalized communities and course-correct along the way. The executive team should understand their industry's pitfalls to make the vision realistic.

Finally, the executive team is responsible for translating the vision to their functional area and measuring progress. This is why a high-functioning executive team is so critical; they'll know what excellence looks like for their own group.

Values

Values are defined as the principles that drive company operations. They add meaning to work and can also serve as guard rails for behaviors, language, and beliefs. For example, if someone values integrity, they will exhibit that through their behavior by owning up to a mistake instead of shirking responsibility or blaming someone else.

How we respect or undermine company values depends on our cycle of socialization. Many people have grown up with a family that valued keeping secrets within the family unit. So even if the company says they value accountability, employees may avoid reporting a manager misbehaving through sexual harassment, microaggressions, or racial discrimination. They've been conditioned since childhood to value the privacy of their "family," in this case their team, and not share what happens with anyone outside of that unit. The C-suite must dogmatically embody company values because even small missteps could be perceived as permission for employees to completely dismiss them. It's not unreasonable to demand a higher level of accountability from the C-suite. If they can't fully and consistently embody the values, then they don't need to be on the executive team. That should be nonnegotiable because anything less sends the wrong message.

There are three types of values:
- Stated values: an expressed principle that has been socialized throughout the company.
- Aspirational values: the evolved version of a stated value that has not been realized in the company.

- Shadow values: the underbelly of the stated value, which reflects its shortcomings and potential toxicity.

The stated value is an expression of what the company knows the company needs to show the world. Every company has stated values, and they often match the rhetoric of industry peers. The shadow values reflect where the company's culture and design undermine stated values in practice. These are unavoidable simply because human nature prioritizes patterns and conformity; we will fiercely adhere to a behavior until it becomes too costly to continue. The aspirational values reflect the next level we stretch into as a company. They keep our principles growing and evergreen.

One common value among tech companies is innovation, so let's use that as an example of a stated value. The shadow of constant innovation could be valuing newness over stability. Constantly developing new ideas instead of perfecting existing ones can lead to creative burnout for employees and change burnout for customers. Eventually, everyone will need some stability. An aspiration of innovation could be seeking self-actualization. Many companies chase being "better" than what competitors have already accomplished. When Instagram came out with Stories, Twitter then developed a similar feature called Fleets. It failed fairly quickly, in part, because it didn't capitalize on the core reasons users love Twitter in the first place. Aspirational values should be focused on how companies can continue to evolve into the best version of their core product, rather than simply chasing competitors.

Viscosity

Viscosity is a scientific concept of the measure of a fluid's resistance to flow based on how thick or free-flowing a liquid is. In other words, it's the pace of movement when facing opposition. High viscosity means high resistance and a slower pace; whereas, low viscosity means less resistance and a faster pace. All companies and industries have a natural pace. Some are fast-paced, like consumer goods, because people make purchases frequently. Others have a slower pace, such as government agencies, because the competing interests of constituents and the bureaucratic red tape subvert frantic change.

The executive team must calculate and manage viscosity to ensure the right systems, processes, and people are in place. It is too costly to rush or lag behind. If we have a competent sales team that is responsive to leads, an intuitive marketing team with catchy campaigns, and an agile product team with a fast turnaround, the company will maintain a quick pace and low viscosity. However, if we have an outdated payment system that takes a week for sales to be approved, the pace slows due to high resistance. In this case, it would be the responsibility of the Chief Financial Officer to fix the issue, but that responsibility can and will shift depending on where the bottleneck is.

Verticals

Verticals are the segmentation of a company's products and services or lines of business. This "V" is a founder favorite. We seek agility and responsiveness to market shifts in an attempt to stay in business. In reality, verticals have a symbiotic relationship with the other three V's. Determine the vision, values, and viscosity of the company before breaking the company into verticals.

Each vertical will have different staffing, technology, and support needs. Verticals can further the founder and executive team's evolution to equity by providing opportunities to address intersectional concerns. Do consumers with disabilities need a specialized product or service? That could be a vertical. Do various age groups or family sizes need high-touch consulting services or product add-ons? That could be a vertical too. On the employee side, verticals are an excellent way to spotlight emerging talent through stretch projects, which are new assignments designed to grow their skills and visibility. We can also leverage cross-vertical work to boost retention and employee engagement. Verticals are where we can be most creative in embedding PCI into the company.

Challenges

Founders usually start a company with a homogeneous group of people. Either we came from the same previous company or school, or we're the same race, gender, and socioeconomic class. Sometimes we might even bring on our family members. We have some important aspects of our identity in common with the starting team, and that fact alone creates deep blind spots that can be almost impossible to overcome without external intervention.

A PCI blind spot is an area on the evolution journey where we cannot see our own bias or the impact of that bias in our ecosystem. Just like a car's blind spot, the closer we are to the executive team, the less we can see them. Now, multiply that by all the dimensions of identity. We suddenly have about 50 cars in our blind spot. We're just moving around, making money, and "changing the world," but we're not even fully aware of what's changing or how it could be so much better.

We might be unmotivated to upend these dynamics because we get a number of psychosocial rewards, such as belonging and validation, from creating homogenous leadership groups. Remember, the purpose of an executive team is to distribute labor, ensure quality, and accelerate progress. Founders tend to feel this is easier with people we already have stuff in common with because we don't have to explain everything or bridge differences. What would normally take two weeks can get done in three days because we have our cousin, our friend from undergrad, or our former coworker on our side. They already get us and don't need as much detail. In PCI work, that homogeneity can be our Achilles' heel.

Chapter 8: Executive Team Impact

It is part of the founder's role to be the organization's equity thermostat. Thermostats set the temperature, unlike a thermometer which simply measures the existing temperature. The organization's temperature is the relationship and interdependence of the four Vs and how we, as founders, set them. Because it's our company, we are responsible for setting those four Vs at the highest level. Understanding the C-suite team dynamics is determined by how willing and capable we are to have that master level of control. Those dynamics can improve or diminish the C-suite's three primary impacts: organization theory, organizational effectiveness, and their relationship with the founder.

Applied Organizational Theory Impact

Organizational theory, or <u>org theory</u>, is an academic understanding of how organizations form, change, and sustain themselves. Org theory posits that organizations are organisms, distinct from humans, systems, and the outputs influencing them. Political and legal changes in the 1980s caused people to begin seeing organizations as their own entities rather than just a result of human influence. Applied organizational theory today is the result of private conversations in the psychology field now becoming a part of the public lexicon.

At its core, org theory is the intersection of psychology, sociology, and anthropology.
- Psychology: the study of how human thoughts and behaviors can influence their lived experiences.
- Sociology: the study of the way humans interact with external environments and influence behavior and thought in group settings.

- Anthropology: the study of what makes an organization a unified group versus a bunch of people who just happen to be in the same place or under the same company name.

There are four types of org theories: classical, neoclassical, contingency, and modern systems. Classical organizational theory is highly structured and hierarchical and hinges on a clear division of labor and processes. Developed at the outset of the Industrial Era, classic organizational theory views people as inputs and as machines. Their work could be judged based on their outputs, and the output quantity and quality determined organizational fit.

When this theory was considered to be too bureaucratic, we moved into human relations theory, or neoclassical theory. This theory involves the psychosocial impacts and inputs of the work. People are no longer viewed as just computers or machines. They're humans, and they deserve to feel good at work. This theory encourages organizations to reflect on these questions: Are we motivating people? Are we rewarding people? Are we providing them with a sense of belonging? This is where we become dependent on less rational inputs such as leadership style, collaboration, etc.

Contingency theory is a hybrid approach. There is an understanding of the need to have structure, but the purpose of the structure is to simplify decision-making. According to this theory, the people who are higher up in the chain of command have more impact on the organization, and as a result, their control should lead to making more rational decisions. The higher up you are, the less emotional you can afford to be because your decisions are too important for you to be reliant on psychosocial factors.

Lastly, the modern system theory centers on deep connectivity between organizational components, which creates an organizational identity. Just like our bodies have different parts working together in systems, modern system theory is the same way. It has multiple management development approaches and is largely based on the quantitative and behavioral sciences.

These org theories impact our capability as the founder because our view of the organization determines who we hire, how we hire, what we encourage, and what we dissuade. Likewise applied org theory reflects the beliefs of the executive team too.

Organizational Effectiveness Impact

Organizational effectiveness implies that a strong executive leadership team makes culture change more efficient. It's simpler to scale and easier to communicate, and everyone finds more satisfaction because there is a sound decision-making structure. There are three major impacts of org effectiveness: employee satisfaction, culture adoption, and scalability acceleration.

Employee Satisfaction

I often surprise startup CEOs when I tell them employee satisfaction is the company's responsibility. Employee satisfaction includes development and growth, realistic job duties and workload, and equitable distribution of rewards and recognition. There are no formal rules or laws to inform a C-suite how much responsibility they should take for the development and training of their employees, but successful companies *are* responsible for a significant portion of employee development. The founder needs to decide how much they are willing to allocate for professional development, surveys, data collection, consultants, tuition reimbursement, training, and conference attendance. If a founder decides they are not going to subsidize these things in terms of money and time, then employees will be less motivated to stay at the company or to apply what they're learning on their own time and money for the benefit of the company.

The executive team is also responsible for creating a realistic job description. If we hire someone to be an engineer, we need to be clear if there are any other job functions or tasks they will need to complete. This includes laying out the less popular expectations of

G&A (general and administrative) functions like finance or HR. This sounds like common sense, but you'd be shocked to discover how many people are working an entirely different job than the one they were hired to do. When I worked for the City of New York, this was called working "out-of-title" and was grounds for a union complaint and/or lawsuit.

Finally, the C-suite boosts employee satisfaction through equitable rewards and recognition. It becomes immediately apparent who is an exec's favorite, which can be demoralizing for the rest of the team. Each functional area in the company will have a different measure of what excellent output looks like; however, the C-suite must ensure appropriate recognition when *any* employee displays excellence. This can include monetary, verbal, and psychosocial rewards and recognition.

Culture Adoption

There's a concept in organizational development created by Peter Senge called a "learning organization," which includes systems thinking, mental models, shared vision, team learning, and personal mastery. Becoming a learning organization is an ideal state because we want employees to be highly agile and focused on continuous improvement to scale faster.

Culture adoption is a critical factor in becoming a learning organization. Our understanding of organizational culture compounds with each professional experience such as school or work. If this is an employee's tenth job, nine other cultures have shaped their view of what the employee experience should look like. As a startup, we need people to adopt the culture we have created. How we build our C-suite shapes how we become a learning organization because it determines how quickly and effectively people will adopt the company's culture.

Both crises and celebrations test cultural adoption. If our culture really is what we say it is, we should be able to pass that test. The C-suite is responsible for making sure the people in their individual functional areas can do that too. Most importantly, employees exemplify culture and learning adoption in the daily decisions they make toward their work and one another.

Scalability Acceleration

Scalability acceleration is the idea that we should be able to make it through the stages of a startup's growth, either on time or faster if our C-suite is effective. If the earliest projection says it should take two years, but we have a highly talented and highly engaged C-suite, we may be able to do it in 18 months or better.

Accelerating scalability requires inspiration, motivation, and collaboration within the C-suite. The C-suite should inspire people to work hard, whether it's because of their charismatic personality, their highly skilled nature, or their ability to manage money. They should make people want to be a part of what they're doing. They should be engaged enough to collaborate effectively. The C-suite team members should be willing to get their hands dirty with the employees rather than barking orders if it means taking them to the next level. It might take some late nights and hard work on the part of the C-suite to really get things done. All of this affects the company's scalability.

Impact on the Founder

Having a high-functioning and synergistic C-suite means we, as founders, get to actually enjoy our company instead of always running from one fire drill to the next. Even today, this is something I am still learning in my own business. Not having the right support means every functional area is not maximizing its potential and is therefore minimizing my own joy. Each functional area of a company has its own best practices. I may have someone on my team who is really good at certain tasks and can do them with their eyes closed. I may think this person is completely invested in the work I'm doing, but that's not always the case. When that happens, I can feel there is a level of excellence missing, but I can't always pick up the slack for them. I can't be expected to do everything in my own company. This is why we hire great people.

I don't have time to do sales, social media management, and video editing in my company. I need to make sure we are hitting our KPIs and paying our bills, but there still needs to be a level of excellence in each of those areas so I've had to hire people to perform those tasks. Likewise, your focus needs to be on sustaining your company, not wondering whether or not someone processed payroll this week, which is what you have a CFO for. When you're missing these pieces and you have to do it all, this limits your scalability.

As a founder, some of this is managing our own past traumas around work and relationships because many of our hesitations and fears may be connected to childhood experiences. There is often a fear that if we don't hurry up and figure something out, it's all going to fall apart. We resort to a "the sky is falling" mentality and only think about how long it will take us to recover, but in reality, it may not be as bad as we think it is. If we have the right C-suite in place, those people can provide us with some of the emotional support we need so we don't have to resort to all the doomsday predictions. These people can help us see other options and keep us level-headed in times of crisis. They're not responsible for controlling these issues for us, but they can be effective in alleviating some of them.

Chapter 9: Executive Team Roles

When C-level executives take accountability for bad behaviors, this elevates PCI to the same level of importance as other company functions like finance or legal. It encourages founders to question what policies we have in place to prevent those behaviors and holds the C-suite accountable. Instead of firing the intern who may have clicked the enter button on a transphobic ad, it means holding the CMO accountable for allowing that content to be put out in the company's name. If we want to say PCI is important to your startup, we need to treat it the same as you would every other function that has severe consequences attached to it. Founders hire the executive team for obvious and hidden reasons. These reasons correspond to the founder's needs - emotional, financial, physical, and mental. Sometimes the reason is the person has a different skill set than the founder; sometimes it's because they do the founder's dirty work quietly. Regardless of the reason, every employee operates in three different roles: functional, operational, and social.

Role	Contributes To	Expiration Date	Relies On
Functional	Organizational structure, goals	Yes	Past experience; potential
Operational	Team workflows and processes	Yes	Volunteers; unconscious bias
Social	Team synergy and viscosity	No	Founder ego; unconscious bias

Functional Roles

The functional role is the person's contribution to the company's structure and the stated job title for which they were hired. In other words, this is what the role should accomplish for the company and includes major projects, roles, tasks, and job titles. This role can also have an expiration date as a result of getting a promotion or being moved to another functional role. It relies on past experience and/or potential.

These are the top roles in the company. At the C-suite level, the focus is on designing, strategizing, and creating structure. In most cases, they will not be responsible for the actual implementation and operational work. They have direct reports to do that. For example, I would never expect my CTO to also be the person sitting down to write the code, so I shouldn't expect my CHRO to do the recruiting. Strategic work requires a separate role from operational work.

C-Suite Role	Abbreviation	Description/Responsibilities
Chief Executive Officer/ President	CEO	The top executive in the company who manages the rest of the C-suite. This person may be different from the founder.
Chief Financial Officer	CFO	Responsible for the company's financial operations and portfolio, budget, and investment strategy.
Chief Administrative Officer	CAO	Responsible for non-operations functional areas, such as HR and finance.
Chief Operations Officer	COO	Responsible for overseeing company outputs, such as research & development and operations.
Chief of Staff	CoS	Acts as an intermediary between the C-suite and the CEO for communications and day-to-day operations.
Chief Marketing Officer	CMO	Responsible for designing consumer brands, retention, and campaign strategies.
Chief Human Resources Officer/ Chief People Officer	CHRO/CPO	Responsible for the design and oversight of all people, culture, and strategy, including workforce planning and compliance.
Chief Diversity Officer/ Head of DEI	CDO	Responsible for designing, implementing, and measuring organization-wide inclusion and representation strategies.
Chief Technology Officer	CTO	Responsible for overseeing the information systems used to run operations and research new technology.
Chief Product Officer/ Head of Product	CPO	Responsible for the strategic product direction.
Chief Legal Officer/ General Counsel	CLO	Head lawyer for the company.
Chief Experience Officer	CXO	Responsible for overseeing customer support and user experience functions.

When I work with clients of startups, I often find myself telling them they need more chief roles. A lot of them want to argue it's not necessary for a startup of their size, and none of their peers have that. This is when I have to break it to them that this is why those peer companies are failing or wasting time putting out fires. They all experience issues down the line, whether it's with retention or organizational structure, because they failed to establish a sizable C-suite from the beginning. This is why it's so necessary to work on organizational structure and role clarity early on.

Operational Roles

The operational role is the value they add to the company's workflows and processes. This is the level of structure they bring, which goes beyond their functional role. This includes administrative team tasks and daily upkeep for the team. Operational roles may have an expiration date, and they rely on volunteers or unconscious biases. One example of this is how women usually take on the role of housekeeping tasks on teams, so they may be responsible for organizing reports, scheduling team meetings, or transcribing meeting minutes.

Dr. Meredith Belbin created a framework of nine box team roles; I use it to describe the different roles people play which contributes to the team and company's workflows. I will use examples from pop culture to illustrate the character traits of each operational role. You may be familiar with some of these characters, and others you may not, but the characteristics of each should be relatable.

Resource Investigator

The resource investigator is someone who is outgoing, enthusiastic, and inquisitive. They find new ideas and bring them back to the team. Tom Sawyer is a resource investigator because he has a big imagination and a sense of adventure inspired by his own inquisitive and exploratory nature. His weakness is that he is sometimes overly optimistic, can easily lose interest in tasks he was once excited about, and may forget to follow up on things.

Team Worker

The team worker is perceptive, diplomatic, and averts friction. They use their versatility to identify the work required and complete it on behalf of the team. Chuckie Finster from *Rugrats* is a team worker because he is always trying to keep the peace and just wants everyone to get along. He can be indecisive in tough situations and tends to avoid confrontation. Team workers might be hesitant to make unpopular decisions because they don't like to go against the grain.

Coordinator

The coordinator focuses on the objectives, draws out team members, and delegates work appropriately. They are mature, confident, and able to identify talent and clarify goals. Gandalf from *The Lord of the Rings* is a coordinator because he is good at assigning tasks and bringing in the right talent. Because he is too often looking at the big picture, he's not always fully present for what needs to happen. Coordinators can be seen as manipulative and might over-delegate tasks, giving the impression they don't want to do their share of the work.

Plant

The plant is highly creative and good at problem-solving in an unconventional way. They are imaginative, free-thinking, and have the ability to generate ideas and solve difficult problems. A good example of this is Raven Baxter from *That's So Raven*. She is often too preoccupied to communicate effectively and avoids incidentals, which is how she ends up getting in trouble in the show. Plants are often absent-minded and forgetful.

Monitor Evaluator

The monitor evaluator is someone who provides a logical eye, makes impartial judgments where required, and weighs up the team's options in a dispassionate way. They are strategic and discerning. Link from *The Matrix* is a monitor evaluator because he's very logical in terms of his skills and knowing what to do to take action. He doesn't trust other people around him though, so he can be overly critical, slow to make decisions, and lack the ability to inspire others on the team. He questions everything, but his sheer skill and drive to be productive make him a great contributor in times of crisis.

Specialist

The specialist brings in-depth knowledge in a very specific area to the team. They are single-minded, self-starting, and might overload you with information. Penelope Garcia from *Criminal Minds* is a specialist because she is the technical analyst for the Behavioral Analysis Unit, so her area of expertise is hyper-specific. She tends to contribute on a narrow front and dwells on technicalities because that's where her role shines.

Shaper

The shaper provides the team with the drive to keep them moving and does not lose focus or momentum. Lennie Briscoe from *Law & Order* is a shaper because he is quick-witted and sharp. He thrives on pressure and loves to provoke people, which can either encourage them to overcome obstacles or offend them. Shapers are usually very focused and risk becoming aggressive and irate in their attempts to get things done.

Implementer

The implementer is practical, reliable, and efficient. They need a workable strategy they can carry out as efficiently as possible. Little Foot from *The Land Before Time* is an implementer in his plan to look for his mother. Like most implementers, Little Foot is inflexible and refuses to listen to other perspectives, which makes him slow to respond to new possibilities.

Completer/Finisher

The completer/finisher is most effective when brought in at the end of tasks to polish and fine-tune the work. They have high standards of quality control. A good example of this role is Nigel from *The Devil Wears Prada* because he polishes and perfects Miranda's designs. However, he can be inclined to worry unnecessarily and is reluctant to delegate. Completers/finishers can often be accused of taking perfectionism to the extreme.

Social Roles

The social roles are what a person contributes to the team's synergy and dynamic in terms of how they interact and make decisions. These include cognitive and emotional needs. Social roles usually don't have an expiration date, and it's difficult for a person to rebrand themselves once they are characterized into a particular role. These roles rely on unconscious bias as well as the founder's ego. Social roles often reinforce bias and stunt others' growth, if not managed carefully. I am going to explain the eight social roles, their value-adds and shadow qualities, and use references from pop culture just as I did for the operational roles.

The Coddler

The coddler is the person to whom the leader whines. Sam Gamgee from *The Lord of the Rings* is a coddler who pacifies Frodo's immaturity. Frodo gets to grow up on Sam's back, and Sam plays a huge role by affirming Frodo's bravery throughout their journey in spite of constant rejection. The key personality traits of the coddler are loyalty and the affirmation of their leader's traits, whether they are good or bad.

Their shadow traits lie in allowing themselves to be an emotional garbage can for the leader and lacking autonomy. They respond primarily to the leader's whims, so they never get to see who they are without the influence of another person. Because teams thrive on being able to understand everybody's individual role, employees might not fully understand the coddler's role since they are only showing up as "leader junior" instead of themselves.

The Challenger

The challenger is the person who is always able to confront and call out other perspectives. Rich Porter from *Paid in Full* was a challenger. He was everything you imagine a drug dealer should *not* be, but he's very successful nonetheless. He's deeply family-oriented, giving, loyal, and protective of people. Because of this, he had a knack for gracefully calling things out he saw in Ace, the main character and narrator. The challenger is confrontational but compassionate, deeply intuitive, and multi-dimensional.

On the shadow side, they can come across as manipulative and/or naive. Because they're confronting what may lie under a mask, they can often rub people the wrong way. They can also be naive to just how sinister people can be. You can trust their positive intentions though. Though Rich Porter was bringing people into the drug game, he was doing it with the intention of giving people money to be able to eat, feed their families, and enjoy life. He really had good intentions and a pure heart. Challengers' motives aren't based on self-aggrandizement, and they don't challenge the founder to embarrass, humiliate, or undermine them.

The Foil

While the challenger confronts the leader with compassion, the foil is the person who confronts the leader with the opposite viewpoint in a more hardcore way. They may cuss you or use sarcasm or disrespect to get you to come around to their side or get the leader's attention. If you tell them to do one thing, they will do the exact opposite for no other reason than to just be different. These people are combative and (seemingly) emotionally detached. John Bender from *The Breakfast Club* is a foil. The foil typically shares similar styles and personality traits with the founder, but the foils feel superior.

Their shadow traits are often being emotionally unaware, sometimes to the point of emotional abuse, and they make work environments feel tense, especially environments that thrive on consensus. Ironically, they reflect the shadow side of the leader that the leader is trying to hide, but it's important for the leader to recognize they are there for a reason.

The Jester

The jester is the person who brings joy to the team but is irresponsible. They act like everything is a joke and don't take anything seriously. Their key personality trait is providing comedic and lighthearted relief. They can mirror back the leader's inner child, which can be incredibly useful in a work environment for relieving intense pressure.

On the shadow side, they can be dismissive of more analytical types, which you need on your team as well, and they can't be trusted with outcomes. A good example of the jester is Shaggy from *Scooby Doo* because his irresponsible actions bring comedic relief to the show, which can be tense and scary at times. We often see him dismiss Fred, who is much more analytical and logical. This dismissive attitude leaves Shaggy and his team members in bad situations they might not have been in otherwise.

The Twin

The twin is the person who almost fully agrees with the founder's views. Twins are very effective at helping the company to accelerate in its early stages because they are low friction, meaning they don't argue or cause conflict. The twin is also great for a founder because they share some of the burdens of the company, so the founder does not burn out with unnecessary stress from feeling like they have the weight of the world on their shoulders. The founder feels like they have an ally in the twin.

The twin's shadow side has a function of codependency, so it doesn't empower the founder or the twin to self-actualize based on their individual needs. While everyone else wants to do their own thing and grow, the twin will shrink themselves to match the founder. Oftentimes, this identity can breed resentment because there is a power dynamic at play. Even if the twin is another C-suite member, the founder still has more power and the twin may not get the same rewards or benefits as the founder. Eli Thompson from *Boardwalk Empire* is the twin of his brother Nucky. At the beginning of the series, Eli agreed with everything Nucky did and said. When Eli discovered he had different needs from his brother, the inner conflict tore him apart.

The Pit Boss

The pit boss maintains the social structure and commands respect. They are the final authority regarding disagreements and requests. Though we hate to admit it, people need someone who they fear. They need someone who they are afraid to cross in the leadership team because everybody won't always be operating from a place of altruism and integrity, especially when it comes to PCI work. Ace Rothstein from *Casino* is a literal and figurative pit boss. Pit bosses have a high level of emotional intelligence and can be incredibly diplomatic. They are great social translators and excel at dealing with all types of personalities to get people to fall in line. They are so good at it that they can make people think it was their idea.

The shadow side is that they often attract people who are users because they're so busy trying to manage and interpret other people's needs that they ignore their own emotional and social needs. In *Casino*, Ace winds up falling in love with a shady woman who ends up being his downfall. She was the one person who was able to interpret him and get him emotionally caught up, which was his Achilles' heel. Founders can support the pit boss by making sure they create personalized development plans for them to focus on, which can prevent them from ignoring their own needs.

The Empath

The empath is responsible for feeling through the leader's emotions. In a positive way, they're able to help the founder maintain a neutral public image. They can help them seem less volatile, more intellectual, and more thoughtful than they might actually be. Because the empath is essentially the founder's emotional therapist, they help the founder feel through all of that stuff. The founder can scream and yell when they talk to the empath, although not necessarily at them, so they can appear emotionally in control to others. Joan Holloway Harris from *Mad Men* is the empath. Though she is a strong female character, she plays the empath role to the men at the firm, allowing them to yell at her and express their true emotions so they can come off as strong and capable in the workplace.

On the shadow side, the empath can often self-destruct through a victim mentality. It's very difficult for empaths to take accountability until they evolve because they feel like everything is happening to them and believe they have less control than they actually do. Because they feel through the leader's emotions, they might say they couldn't accomplish or finish a task because they knew the leader was upset. It's hard for them to separate their own feelings from someone else and pay attention to the tasks at hand. They can also experience burnout easier than any other social role.

The Shock Absorber

Finally, there is the shock absorber, who absorbs the leader's pressure and acts as a buffer so the founder isn't forced to absorb all the impact from volatility. They differ from the jester because they are not irresponsible, but they're also not the coddlers because they don't absolve the leader from their responsibilities. This person strictly exists to take the punch. They can easily be taken for granted in ways the other roles are not; in fact, they can often be invisible. The founder may not respect the shock absorber, but they are keeping the founder out of all types of difficulties in the company. They add value by keeping relationships calm.

The shock absorber's shadow trait is allowing themselves to be dehumanized because they end up being more like a punching bag. Annie Johnson from *Imitation of Life* is the consummate shock absorber for her daughter by playing along with being referred to as the maid so her daughter could deny her identity as a person of color born to a Black mother. Her mother suffered throughout her life, so as to not ruin the life her daughter created for herself. Shock absorbers may not get the same development opportunities as other people because the founder doesn't really respect them in the same way they do other roles.

Roles in Action

Each role type doesn't exist in a bubble. The three types work in tandem, leading to a persona within the company. Sometimes the functional, operational, and social roles complement one another; other times, they contrast one another in harmful ways. Here is an example. You implore the CFO to conduct a pay equity study because Asian women employees have filed complaints about being underpaid in comparison to their white male counterparts. The CFO is a specialist operationally and a foil socially, so he refuses to conduct the study explaining the months of research it took to make the existing compensation framework and complains the existing pay scales, and any subsequent pay inequities, were your idea. You quickly realize this issue will need another voice and ask your CHRO for support. The CHRO is a team worker operationally and an empath socially; she has faced the brunt of employees' complaints to HR on pay equity. The CHRO feels torn on how to balance employees' need for transparency and fairness with the CFO's feeling of being sabotaged on the compensation framework he's most proud of implementing. She defers to whatever you and the CFO decide but offers to write the all-staff communication on the decision. You stall on what to do next.

No one said being a founder would be easy. These dilemmas occur all the time in PCI work because of the complexities that result as each team member acts out each of their three roles. It's your responsibility to understand which roles each of your C-suite team members are playing and how their roles are impacting you and the organization.

Titles & Levels

One of the primary steps in an organization's evolution to equity is examining titling and leveling. While we've spent this chapter discussing executive team roles, they are only the beginning. Clear levels and titles eliminate so much confusion in PCI processes. The executive team should set levels before picking titles because levels clarify responsibility, authority, and desired impact. Appropriate leveling creates the skeleton of the PCI workflows. For example, only director-level titles can approve expenses above $100,000, and program managers should be creating training schedules. It's important to put responsibility where it's supposed to be to avoid playing hot potato with PCI responsibilities.

Leveling, or job classification, defines job tasks, task groupings, areas of responsibility, and the mutually beneficial value for a particular role and clarifies the direction of accountability. If a company puts out a racist ad approved by the CMO, it's the CMO's fault, not the writer's. The CMO should have processes and systems in place to avoid injuring the company's brand.

Once we define the level, we can then select a job title. Job titles signal to others the role's prestige and importance. Sometimes, we can appropriately level someone but give them a job title that doesn't feel senior enough so people won't respect them. The founder should develop company-wide titling standards, and the company should have consistent titling conventions across the entire organization, including in the C-suite. I see this happen a lot when companies bring in people from marginalized backgrounds, and they may make them the head of a role, like the Head of Product, but everyone else in the company is the Chief of Marketing or Chief of Design. Employees feel confused as to why that person is different, and they assume one role is less important than the other.

It's not as important as you may think to follow trends with titling, especially when the leveling for the job doesn't match up. Calling someone a Chief People Officer instead of Head of HR is less important than empowering that person with the appropriate task groupings and paying them well enough to justify the level of responsibility they have. Those are the parts that actually matter.

Titles and levels are the formal classifications, or what's written on paper, but the founder also has a shadow team. These are the people who we look to when things need to get done. If our shadow team is not the C-suite, then we are engineering inequity in the company. This could either mean our C-suite is ineffective in PCI and our shadow team is effective, so the shadow team does the work without glory. Or, it could mean our C-suite is really effective in this work, but our shadow team is deeply biased and able to quietly influence the destruction of the PCI efforts we're currently putting into place.

Chapter 10: Ignorance as a Roadblock

Founders and executive teams have areas of expertise they leverage to build the company. While they can't be an expert in everything, there are certain areas where ignorance can be especially detrimental. PCI is one of them. The detriment primarily stems from PCI initiatives that feel disjointed and irrelevant to the executive's functional work. Whether it's a recruiting partnership, launching a new manager's training program, or a targeted advertising campaign, PCI work should matter to the bottom line. Executive ignorance is most detrimental to establishing role clarity, recognizing bias, and meeting compliance needs.

Role Clarity

Every C-suite role has a function in PCI. When people feel constrained in any particular task or deliverable, they lean into the worst parts of themselves such as biases, microaggressions, and stereotypes. If you know there is a budget constraint on a marketing campaign, you would likely avoid hiring an external marketing agency to check your ad to make sure it's not racist toward the Indigenous community. This choice puts the company at risk of a lawsuit or lost revenue through consumer rejection.

All three areas of PCI are the C-suite's responsibility. Role clarity in PCI helps the C-suite personalize PCI work for their functional area and cross-pollinate where needed to increase impact. Startups typically have small executive teams at the start, so they have to scale their C-suite team the same way they would with their revenue. Once we have a clear view of each person's knowledge, skills, abilities, and interests, we can then invest in their learning and development or hire external consultants to shore up the PCI-related gaps.

One solution is to invest in emerging leaders but hire an external consultant during the growth process to provide coverage. I often provide this coverage for my startup clients as a fractional executive. Role elasticity helps identify emerging leaders by allowing lower-titled employees to work on stretch projects to grow the necessary skills for a C-suite role. You can see who on your team is showing promise and has the knowledge, skills, ability, and interest to fill it. If this is done right, it can be a company morale booster, but if it's done wrong, it can look like favoritism. Be sure to provide equal opportunities for visibility and performance assessment so the growth process is fair.

Bias

Everyone has biases, even if their identity includes marginalized traits in a dimension. Ignorance of these biases opens the company to legal vulnerabilities such as lawsuits, poor employer brand ratings and turnover, and low-quality products and services. There are several types of bias, but there are several specific types that are more likely to pop up for the C-suite: affinity bias, attribution bias, beauty bias, confirmation bias, and conformity bias.

Affinity bias is based on the idea that if someone shares our dimensional identity traits, we are more likely to gravitate toward them. However, if someone is different in the dimensions of identity that matter most to us or we have been taught to prioritize, then we won't bring them in close to us.

Attribution bias means likeability can make an executive untouchable in our organizations. Attribution bias leads us to underestimate the person we have a bias toward, and this shows up in two ways. If we have an executive who we have always favored, we may underestimate the negative impact they have on the rest of the team. Alternatively, if we have an executive who is always doing our dirty work, we may underestimate them in a negative way by taking joy in the idea that our team is afraid of them. This comes up a lot in companies, particularly in HR. Spineless leaders will activate HR leaders who are thirsty for power as their bulldog, an agent of terror to make other employees scared to push for inclusion.

Beauty bias shows favoritism toward the conventionally attractive and punishes those who are considered less attractive. Every culture has its own beauty ideals, whether it be height, weight, hair color, eye color, or any other trait of appearance. Issues like colorism (skin tone discrimination), featurism (race-centered body discrimination), and texturism (hair discrimination) associate intelligence and competence with certain qualities. Height and body weight also contributes to beauty bias.

Confirmation bias reinforces what we already want to believe. If we believe someone who graduated from Harvard or Yale is extremely intelligent when it comes to structuring a company, then we already value their opinion over anyone else's. We might ask that person a question about our company, and they might have one good insight, and we immediately say, "See, I told you Harvard or Yale has the smartest people." That thought is a confirmation bias because we are reinforcing what we already want to believe.

On the other hand, *conformity bias* is towards anyone who disagrees with what we already believe. In any C-suite, there has to be a level of groupthink in order for the team to get anything done. We only tolerate disagreement so far before it becomes an unhelpful distraction. The goal is acceleration, so the person disagreeing only has so many "but what about"s before they're expected to fall in line with the majority.

All of these types of biases point back to the founder. It's easy to villainize our C-suite, but as founders, we hired them and empower them, which makes us responsible for their biases. It's our job to recognize where the bias concentrates on the team and begin correcting these behaviors before they become cancerous to the company.

Compliance

When it comes to compliance, the consulting giant Deloitte has a DEI maturity model people love, and it's broken down into four stages: compliance, programmatic, leader-driven, and integrated. I'm not a big fan of this model, despite its popularity, because compliance isn't just a passing phase. Compliance is often viewed as an absence of innovation, cohesion, and collaboration. But compliance is not bad – it's necessary throughout the company's evolution journey. Companies need structure, standards, and boundaries. Compliance means having a floor by telling the staff and the world that the company won't go lower than this standard. Our bottom should feature compliance with federal, state, and local laws; performance standards that tie into compensation; and normalized events and participation that bring visibility to marginalized dimensions of identity.

The startup environment is naturally chaotic and in flux as a result of scaling, so they do need a sense of stability somewhere. As founders, we need to have standards for the way we treat people and consequences for when people are mistreated. When companies experience extreme change, we may have a lawsuit on their hands if we don't have structures in place like written policies for filing complaints, an employee handbook, or a code of conduct. All of these "unsexy" things about running a company are necessary. If we don't have them, we run the risk of toppling our whole company.

As a founder, ask yourself, what is my company's floor across the PCI landscape? What is our moral bottom?

Chapter 11: Emotional Intelligence
An Unignorable Elephant

I saved emotional intelligence for last because it requires so much for us to master. Even still, we never truly "arrive" because we have to learn to calibrate in new environments and situations. Up until the last decade or so, society has celebrated a leader's ability to ignore emotions, focus only on the numbers, and be willing to make deep cuts for the sake of the bottom line. We have deprioritized emotional intelligence, connection, and empathy. This deepened our collective equity crisis because we don't honor the totality of our own individual identity. This lack of honor overvalued things like money, revenue, and sales and ignored the human experience. A lack of emotional intelligence is one of the most detrimental roadblocks in our evolution to equity.

Emotional intelligence is an output of social-emotional learning (SEL), which is an integral part of education and human development. SEL is the process through which children and adults acquire and apply the knowledge, skills, and attitudes to develop healthy identities, manage emotions, achieve personal and collective goals, feel and show empathy, establish and maintain supportive relationships, and make responsible and caring decisions. In other words, SEL is the process of developing emotional intelligence and other "soft" skills.

Early researchers of emotional intelligence include Peter Salavoy and John Mayer; the concept was popularized by Dan Goleman in 1995. Since then, it has taken on a life of its own with various assessments and tests that are easily accessible online. Emotional intelligence has five parts: self-awareness, self-management, relational awareness, relationship management, and motivation.

- **Self-awareness** is the recognition of one's own emotional state, including the transitions between emotional states.

- **Self-management** is the application or implementation of effective actions based on self-awareness.
- **Relational awareness** is the understanding of other people's emotional states.
- **Relational management** is the set of actions you take to impact interpersonal dynamics.
- **Motivation** is the drive to explore any of the other areas of emotional intelligence as a result of a potential loss or opportunity.

We are all likely to be stronger in certain areas and weaker in others. Depending on our identity dimensions, we may have been socially conditioned to be stronger in certain areas than others as well. Asian women may be perceived to be really strong in relationship management because they don't lash out at people and may not be aggressive about pushing their own ideas in conversation, but they also may struggle with self-awareness because they weren't taught to acknowledge their own emotions. This is more a function of socialization than personal choice.

Founders hire people for C-suite roles with the assumption they will have been socialized with all the skills needed to thrive in their role, but that assumption isn't true. We don't pay attention to the ways in which the various dimensions of identity play into our ability to thrive or sabotage our C-suite's roles. There is also an expectation among many founders that C-suite leaders need way less development than they actually do, which is also not true. I've had several conversations with clients about this because they hire very talented people, but I hear crickets when I ask about the executive's development plan. There's a shared responsibility for development and growth. The C-suite's commitment to building emotional intelligence will be a signal to the rest of the company about what is permissible and desirable.

Self-awareness means recognizing we were happy at 10:55, but when we saw our boss call at 11, we immediately felt annoyed. Self-awareness does not mean we are taking action though. For people who tend to intellectualize their emotions, self-awareness is often a struggle because they have such a shallow understanding of their emotional state. While self-awareness is still a skill in and of itself, the goal is to be able to self-manage. If we know we are angry, which is self-awareness, self-management is the ability to take a step back to manage that anger properly. If we are on the phone when we feel angry, that could mean ending the call early or changing the subject to something more lighthearted.

Remember, we are talking about the full range of emotions, which means managing positive emotions as well. There are some people who have to carefully measure their happiness around those they don't trust, which means not getting too excited about certain things around others. This also relates to identity dimensions because people who grew up experiencing childhood trauma of some type tend to struggle with establishing and maintaining boundaries with others, whether it's oversharing or a fear of getting too close to people. Just like self-awareness, self-management also includes the full range of emotions. The C-suite in particular has to carefully manage the ways in which they express their emotions. Regardless of what type of leader we actually are, people have perceptions of how leaders should behave and how leaders in particular functional areas should behave. As an example, people may expect the CMO or CPO to be really friendly, tell jokes, and be overall very personable, but people might be miffed if the CFO or chief legal counsel behaved like that. Either way, it's important to remember this doesn't make someone any less effective at their job, but it's a bias people have around personality and job title.

What's important about self-management is its level of effectiveness because it's not just about being effective for other people, but also for ourselves. As founders, we have to manage ourselves in the context of potential biases and perceptions of what a founder should be. The C-suite can support themselves through this by being unified and having their own insulated protections and dynamics. If the C-suite isn't on the same page, the rest of the employees will feel that.

Relational awareness is where the term "reading the room" comes from because it's a blend of intuition and pattern recognition. Let's say I get on a call with someone and plan to get straight into the agenda, but I notice they are looking a little sad. My ability to recognize that is relational awareness. From there, I likely wouldn't jump right into the meeting. Instead, I would stop and take a moment to ask how they're doing. Likewise, if I have someone on my team who I know coaches their son's basketball practice after work one day, I may notice they start trying to wrap up their day by 5 P.M. They may pick up the pace and move a little faster so they can get out of work on time. My ability to recognize those behaviors for what they are, and not that the team member is upset or uninterested, is another way of practicing relational awareness. Just like self-awareness, relational awareness is not the action but the recognition. Once we are able to synthesize the information in a way that brings us to a conclusion, we can take action, which is relational management.

The pandemic actually upended the thin threads of what we thought was relational awareness. When we are in person with each other, sometimes just physical presence can make us feel like we are more relationally aware than we actually are. When everyone went virtual, a lot of leaders struggled because they couldn't feel the energy in the virtual room and couldn't take a pulse on what was happening. As founders, it's our responsibility to strengthen our ability to be relationally aware in these circumstances. We need to work on all of them, but relational awareness is particularly important because it is how we understand those centers of power, privilege, influence, and inequity. If we lack relational awareness, we cannot understand those four dynamics.

While relational awareness is the understanding of others' emotional states, relationship management is the set of actions we take to impact interpersonal dynamics. Sometimes we might want to change them and sometimes we might want to maintain them. If somebody makes a racist remark to someone else, we, as founders, have to step in and say it's inappropriate. If that happens, we need to upend the social dynamics because we want people to tell us what happened and be honest about how it hurt them. There's a lot at play here so we have to be keenly aware of where we are tracking as a credible leader, which is where relational awareness is important. We have to know what's going on and then take effective action.

People are constantly absorbing data points, but the synthesis is where the problem can begin when it comes to equity and PCI work. Some people who are neurodivergent may struggle to synthesize the information they are getting, which can be a struggle for them. There are so many mental health disorders that suppress our ability to interpret our emotions and/or the emotions of others. In some cases, this makes people hypersensitive, which can cause them to misinterpret the data points they are getting. It's important to know what our baseline is, so we can recognize when we are being hypersensitive in our relational awareness, but also aware we aren't becoming apathetic to the emotional states of others. This can also be a danger in leadership, especially because leaders are often socialized into this cultural phenomenon where they don't care about people and just want to get to the bottom line.

The final piece is motivation, which is a pivot point that could occur between any of the other areas of emotional intelligence because they are non-sequential. Motivation can occur in any sequence and any place in the sequence. We've defined the four motivations earlier as money, prestige, self-actualization, and safety, so it could be the motivation to explore any one of these because of a potential loss or opportunity. If I think I'm going to get fired because my employee keeps reporting me for cussing them out, that's going to motivate me to be more self-aware. In this case, it's a "let me check myself before I wreck myself" situation, and I might choose to go to therapy. Perhaps this behavior stems from alcoholism or anger issues rooted in childhood trauma. It's important to recognize how our childhood and cycle of socialization have impacted our experiences and behaviors as founders. That may be what motivates us to become better at self-management.

Our role, as founders, is to build our own emotional intelligence while guiding and supporting the executive team to build theirs too. This is one of your most important job tasks. Every other aspect of the executive team, from purpose to impact, relies on emotional intelligence. As the C-suite blossoms into an emotionally intelligent, high-functioning team, the organization will bloom too.

PCI for Your Organization

We're the founders of dynamic organizations, and that happened because of focus and intentionality. It's time to apply that same focus and intentionality to People, culture, and inclusion (PCI) in your company. As founders, it's our job to make sure PCI work is functioning smoothly and is aligned with the company's vision and values. PCI becomes the thread of the organization - it pulls the team together when executed well and exposes gaps when it's dysfunctional.

I saved this section for last because I wanted you to spend time understanding how you and your senior-most leaders fit into the company. Now, we'll work through each aspect of PCI to define its purpose, assess its value in your organization's current state, and begin choosing where to apply its principles. I expect you'll have some "ouch" and "aha" moments, possibly even some "WTF" reactions as well – all of which are equally valid.

Emocognition is our partner in working through these reactions. Allow the emotional triggers to signal what's important to you, then activate cognitive processes to work towards solutions. We will leverage knowledge, memory, perception, and language to think through what progress can be in our company. This, my fellow founders, requires empathy, critical thinking, and analytical reasoning. This part of the book is more of a textbook, without the homework. Keep a journal nearby to note where you're making progress and where you haven't even started moving yet. Most importantly, keep in mind the actions you will need to take in each area and analyze where you need to involve others. PCI starts and ends with the founder. Use this section to begin the action planning process for the company.

Chapter 12: The Equity Ecosystem

Equity is defined as an enduring condition of sameness in access, opportunity, and experience. While equity hinges on sameness, it requires varying levels of intervention and investment to realize. If we decide to focus on creating an equitable experience for employees with disabilities, we will have to invest more money into equipment for accommodations so they are able to fully participate in meetings to the same degree people without disabilities can. The evolution to equity symbolizes the company's journey to becoming a company where everyone enjoys access, benefits, and visibility. This includes financial benefits, cultural visibility, and access to safety and delight.

Equity is an output. It is the aggregate of a wide range of inputs from the people and organizations we interact with as we grow the company. This is our equity ecosystem. An ecosystem is a network of relationships, where you are both feeding and being fed. Creating an equity ecosystem means building points of connection, managing weak points, and balancing power, privilege, and influence. Relationships are the connections between stakeholders in your ecosystem, and those give-and-take relationships are constantly being rebalanced based on external influences.

The equity ecosystem includes internal and external stakeholders. The company's equity ecosystem extends beyond just the founder's direct-report community. It takes much more than just those at the top to create a healthy environment where everyone can thrive equally. The equity ecosystem includes customers, all employees, investors, community leaders, and political figures too. It is not a circle like the majority of ecosystems we are introduced to in grade school science classes. It's a web where power, privilege, and influence have both direct and indirect impacts on the stakeholders in the ecosystem. In the graphic below, I've illustrated how the equity ecosystem's stakeholders impact one another. Notice there are solid lines where the impact is direct and dashed lines where the impact is indirect.

Both matter because they don't always have to touch us directly in order to affect us.

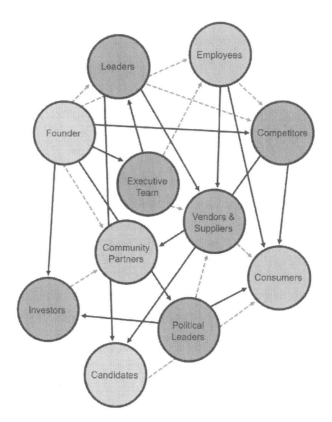

Many new founders try to be socially conscious and naively center on a narrow goal, single issue, or small group to the detriment of others in the ecosystem. Our PCI work should be robust enough to improve the experiences of the entire ecosystem, which is why we need to understand the people and mental maps that drive our evolution strategy. I've developed two tools to help founders gauge an ecosystem's networks: the impact spectrum and the energy matrix. Both tools are useful for categorizing how ecosystem stakeholders may accelerate or slow down PCI work, as well as how they extract from or enhance the organization and its PCI work.

PCI Impact Spectrum

The impact spectrum is where we have champions on one side and blockers on the other. This spectrum is a way of assessing our potential viscosity in PCI work.

- Champions act as helpers and increase the organization's speed. They have the power, influence, resources, and connections to accomplish our PCI goals.
- Blockers act as deep resistors and slow the organization down. Blockers are easily identifiable when they have the power to block, but we may not notice them if they impact quietly through influence.

Blocker   Champion

Champions are visible, credible, and reliable, and they want to see PCI work succeed. While champions can be at any title level, typically the most effective champions are, at a minimum, people managers, but they ideally should be executives or senior leaders within the organization. Because we naturally interact through power and influence dynamics at work, we're more likely to take an executive's efforts seriously than someone who is a lower-leveled individual contributor.

On the other hand, blockers are the people who will actively hinder PCI efforts based on the current iteration or aspiration of the organization's strategy. Blockers are not just people from a majority group; people from marginalized groups can also be blockers. If a Black employee balks at the idea of celebrating Hispanic Heritage Month because they didn't get the celebration they wanted for Black

History Month, they would be a blocker to the PCI strategy for Hispanic community inclusion.

Blocking PCI work doesn't always imply negative intent, but it can still have a negative impact. If your Chief Financial Officer says the company will not fund external consultants to teach people managers how to improve their coaching skills, that person is a blocker. Even if their intention is to save money to ensure the company remains cash positive, they're still blocking the PCI strategy to include expert training voices.

We need both champions and blockers, and both groups have pros and cons. One of the pros to having a PCI champion is credibility because they're trusted by people who are often the beneficiaries of the PCI strategy. Another benefit is the moral support needed to do some pretty difficult work; implementing PCI work, especially in DEI, can be mentally taxing. Champions can provide a listening ear, sound advice, and empathy. The cons of having a champion, especially too many champions, include competing interests between champions or over-championing one dimension to the detriment of others. This happens often with women's initiatives in PCI because white women are likely the most visible marginalized group. It's very easy to do a whole lot of work around women's equity in a company that doesn't honor the intersectional identities of other groups.

We also need to have blockers along our evolution journey. Yes, we *need* them! Their potential resistance increases our viscosity, slowing us down. We can use their resistance to refine our strategy and foolproof the work to avoid giving them any reason to mistrust, sabotage, or ignore it. As irritating as blockers may be, they actually make us better in the long run if we can leverage them appropriately. One of the pros of a blocker is what I call the sandpaper effect. They hone our efforts, just like sandpaper, even if they are irritating at that moment. One major con to having a blocker, especially if they are a particularly high-ranking employee or a person with a lot of influence, is that they can sabotage PCI work before the founder even realizes it. Oftentimes, it's not always a raging inferno but rather a slow burn of confusion, disillusionment, and misinformation that can completely derail our evolution to equity.

Because of intersectionality, it's possible for someone to be both a champion and a blocker, especially when there's no strategy in place. A person may champion something that feels personally important or familiar to them, but they will block something unfamiliar or something they don't really care about. This happens all the time in PCI. Someone may champion pay equity for women, which may overwhelmingly impact white women, but will completely shun the idea of doing anti-racism work or buying accessible resources for employees who have disabilities. We want people to focus on the totality of their identity across all dimensions, so they are able to recognize where their potential blind spots are.

PCI Energy Matrix

The second tool is the PCI energy matrix, which is composed of patrons, sponges, and partners. This tool helps us track where we lose and gain energy for PCI work.

- Patrons are people or entities who give us more than we give to them in return. They are designed to help us grow beyond our limitations by adding more value than we could produce currently by ourselves.
- Sponges are people or entities who we give more to than we receive in return. They help prevent us from becoming too arrogant because they keep us focused on giving back and adding value to others rather than just ingesting and consuming resources.
- Partners are people or entities with whom we have reciprocity, where giving and receiving are nearly equal. This prevents us from focusing too much on transactional relationships and instead has us prioritize relationships that keep us in a state of near equilibrium.

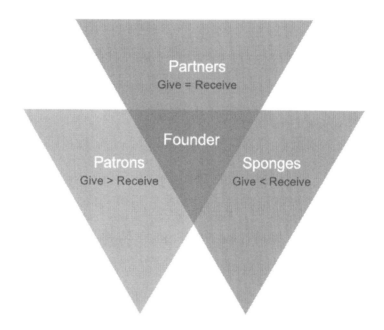

The energy matrix is not quite a sequence like a food chain, where animals are only eating certain foods and not others. It's more complex because energy can be passed at any time and in any order, but it's similar in that we can't feed other people unless we are being fed. Energetic benefits can come in many forms including money, feeling good about ourselves, building stronger relationships, or making connections we might not have otherwise. Take fundraising as an example. Investors are patrons because they are giving way more than they are receiving at first. If founders prioritize investors too much, we ignore the power of philanthropy because enough money is never enough. Conversely, if we focus too much, too early on philanthropy and earn revenue too slowly, we'll become resentful because we cannot sustain the business.

Partner relationships matter too. It's important to develop reciprocal relationships with other organizations because we can both give to and receive from one another in ways that won't leave us feeling overly depleted. Partnering with historically Black colleges and universities (HBCUs) designed to help with learning and career development is one example of this because the HBCU is maturing future talent to help the company scale, and the founder's monetary donations help the HBCU thrive.

In an ideal world, a company could get to the point where they develop an equity ecosystem that has mostly partners, but the key is to balance it out as the company continues to develop. Do you find you have more patrons than sponges? When you do, you fall into a place where your company looks selfish, which can risk concerns like cultural appropriation. The LGBTQ+ community is frequently a patron to organizations, particularly in the fashion and beauty communities. Companies often take the techniques, products, and styles they develop over time without creating talent pipelines, donating to LGBTQ+-focused charities, or advocating for political equity.

It's impossible to avoid having people as partners, patrons, or sponges, and we actually need all three to have a true ecosystem. The founder and executive team should be conscientious of what balance is appropriate for the company and adjust accordingly.

Chapter 13: People

The People aspect of PCI centers on managing the employee lifecycle and strengthening HR functional areas throughout the organization. Managing the employee lifecycle is a product, and strengthening HR is like stockpiling your toolshed to ensure you can always deliver the product. HR, ironically, tends to be an afterthought in a founder's design for the company. We solicit recruiters to hire staff on an ad hoc basis and outsource other tasks like benefits administration and employee analytics and insights. HR service providers bank on founders ignoring the importance of People in the organization, and they are profiting as a result of it.

Ignoring the consequences of subpar People work is a massive failure. These consequences include attrition (staff turnover), disengagement (staff apathy), and lower productivity (staff stagnation). Even if the consequences are cyclical, meaning they rise and fall, the impact on the company's viscosity and vision may be permanent. It's better to prevent the consequences than try to heal them after they spread.

The Employee Lifecycle

The employee lifecycle is a framework for understanding how people move through their tenure in an organization. There are several versions of this framework with as few as four and as many as nine phases. My preferred model includes six phases, and each has different purposes and results.

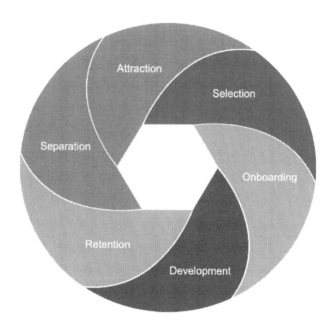

- **Attraction**: Finding talent and introducing them to our employer brand. Attraction should result in mutual curiosity and opportunities for future connection.
- **Selection**: Determining candidates' job fit and strengthening interest. Selection should result in mutual delight and clarity on the value-adds to the candidate and organization.
- **Onboarding**: Integrating the new employee into the organization and the team. Onboarding should result in recouping the selection process investment by teaching cultural and behavioral standards, assigning new hires to meaningful projects, and setting goals with their supervisors.
- **Development**: Investing in employees' skills and well-being. Development should result in preventive and corrective interventions to increase employee satisfaction and productivity.

- **Retention**: Analyzing opportunities for growth and recalibrating organizational fit. Retention should result in employee loyalty and increased mutual delight.
- **Separation**: Disconnecting with grace and retaining mutual respect. Separation should result in the employee and organization receiving feedback, as well as both sides seeing opportunities to improve in the future.

The difficulty in managing the employee lifecycle stems from a few factors including time, money, attention, and presence. Founders have to balance each factor for each employee, and the six lifecycle phases require special care to get the most value. The time factor is most critical during the attraction and retention phases because we're often one decision away from losing great talent. We need to act, and continuously act, quickly to keep talent close. The money factor is most important during the development phase of the lifecycle. Growth is expensive! We need to be bold in how we train, stretch, and recognize the teammates we don't want and can't afford to lose.

Our presence is most needed during the selection and onboarding phases. Studies have shown new hires know if they'll leave the company as early as the initial phone screening and as late as 30 days into a new role. How can we show up meaningfully during this vulnerable period in a candidate/new hire's journey? The answer could be a breaking point for the relationship. Finally, we must pay careful attention during the separation phase. Beyond the obvious concerns of poaching other employees and stealing company secrets or property, separation is our last chance to understand how we can improve the employee experience and show appreciation for what the separating employee has contributed to the team. It can be very difficult to maximize each phase for the entire team because each person may be in a different phase. Plus, there are always competing interests, needs, and motivations.

It is also important to note the lifecycle phases are not just one and done. Employees often re-cycle through the phases if they are promoted, reassigned to a new position as a lateral move, or boomerang back to the company after a hiatus. How we treat employees during this re-cycle can injure our employer brand.

Let's say your company experiences a surge in customers after a new feature launch, so you opt to create a new vertical for premium membership which requires forming a new team of six. You rehire a former teammate for the group's director role, citing a need for someone with wide industry experience, though the rehire was not well-liked in their previous role at your company. You promote two team members – one who is your cousin and the other a relatively new hire with many industry contacts – through an informal selection process. You recruit the remaining three hires from your current staff through a formal 3-step interview process and require their manager's approval before the transfer. The two promotions receive pay increases ranging from 20-45%, and the final three transfers receive no pay increase or title bump. How do you think this will impact team morale, attrition, and employee productivity?

Again, there are consequences for how we handle the employee lifecycle. No one likes to watch others receive the accolades we feel we deserve, and we certainly don't like to watch people hoard raises and bonuses while our salaries and job titles remain stagnant. Founders are the source of inequity and fairness. Our consistency in managing the employee lifecycle means we get a happy, productive team that wants to stick around and grow.

HR Functions

The employee lifecycle is a product, and HR is the toolkit to craft the product. HR has rightfully earned the reputation of being terrible – it has an outdated design, is hard to operate, and produces inconsistent results. I call HR "Legal Junior" because its main purpose at most companies seems to be protecting the organization at all costs. That shouldn't be the case. HR is a mediator and translator between employees and organizational leaders, including the founder. Its role should make the experience for both sides easier.

The Society for Human Resources Management (SHRM) once created a graphic with 6-7 HR functions and their primary contributions. I've since grown in my understanding of HR as a discipline and believe there are 12 HR functional areas. They are:

- **Talent Acquisition**: Owns the attraction and selection process by sourcing talent, building formal recruitment processes, and managing talent databases; manages internal and external job sites and postings; and coordinates social media presence for recruitment purposes.
- **Compensation and Benefits** (also referred to as Total Rewards): Owns all projects and processes related to pay, bonus, and equity; manages the benefits enrollment process and selects vendors as needed; monitors role leveling and titling standards; and co-manages promotion processes and rewards and recognition programs.
- **Learning and Development**: Owns training program design, implementation, and evaluation; manages training and coaching vendor relationships and databases; enforces compliance training across the organization; and co-manages promotion processes and rewards and recognition programs.
- **HR Business Partnership (HRBP)**: Owns people managers and HR relationships; owns workforce planning projections and employee trend identification; and coordinates talent movement implementation (e.g. promotions, internal transfers, and reorganizations).
- **HR Analytics**: Owns the collection and analysis of employee data (e.g. demographics, labor division, and employee experience surveys); and coordinates HR reporting on employee performance, trends, and experiences.
- **HR Information Systems (HRIS)**: Owns HR system vendor relationships and system launches, maintenance, and product/service sunsets (shutdowns).
- **Employee Relations and Compliance**: Owns the development and maintenance of employee policies/handbooks, standard operating procedures (SOPs),

and reporting of compliance standards to regulatory agencies; manages the creation and maintenance of employee complaint procedures, corrective action processes, and employee protection programs; and coordinates employment agreements and collective bargaining agreements.

- **HR Operations**: Owns the day-to-day execution of HRIS processes (e.g. new hire document processing, system activation of title/payroll changes, leave of absence processing); and monitors talent movement in HR systems to ensure compliance and accuracy of workforce data (e.g. reporting structure, pay rates, benefits selections).
- **HR Communications**: Owns all internal messaging for HR in coordination with specific functional areas; maintains employee information sites and channels; and co-designs announcements with team leaders as needed.
- **Risk Management**: Owns the development of employee safety protocols; monitors emerging labor trends and assesses organizational gaps; and maintains relationships with external vendors, influencers, and political leaders to boost the company's employer market position.
- **Diversity and Inclusion***: Owns the design and implementation of employee programs to increase diverse representation, prevent policy violations, and ensure culture adoption; and manages external vendor relationships for diversity and inclusion programs.
- **Organizational Development***: Owns organization design initiatives (e.g. layoffs and reorganizations); introduces relevant research regarding workforce development trends and history; and owns the workforce planning and succession planning processes to ensure coverage for existing and emerging business goals.

*Neither of these definitions are exhaustive enough to describe the depth of the functional areas' impact. We will cover each in more detail in Chapters 14 and 15.

All of the HR functional areas will have some overlap; however, some groups will work more closely with each other than others – I call this the buddy system. When two or more functional areas work together, they lower the organization's viscosity and the company goes further, faster.

Here are some examples of highly effective buddy pairs in HR:

- Risk Management and Employee Relations: This pair protects employees' psychological and physical safety, boosts the company's legal protections, and helps the company avoid unnecessary risks of noncompliance.
- HR Business Partners and HR Analytics: This pair is a data powerhouse. Between the grassroots work of HRBPs and the statistical insights of the HR Analytics team, founders should always have a solid understanding of how employees feel, what they need, and where they're most at risk.
- Compensation and Benefits and Learning and Development: This pair streamlines career movement and can significantly boost retention. They set sensible career levels and job descriptions while ensuring employees are more than prepared to perform at their full potential.
- Talent Acquisition and HR Operations: This pair helps new hires and candidates enjoy the courting process through easy-to-use systems and processes and in-time information to attach themselves to the company.
- Employee Relations and Compliance and Learning and Development: This pair treats problems and then prevents recurrence. They help employees feel comfortable reporting leader and peer missteps and then retrain the team so the issue doesn't happen again.
- HR Information Systems and HR Operations: This pair is the underrated heroes of HR. Every experience employees have with HR runs through a technology system, and this pair ensures those systems work smoothly and are easy to use.

HR isn't all roses and sunshine. Some functional area connections are necessary for overall organizational effectiveness but are incompatible. I call them HR frenemies. This means their goals, workflows, or employee-perceived purpose may not work well with another group.

Here are some HR frenemy pairs:

- HR Analytics and Employee Relations and Compliance: This pair can be perceived as misaligned by employees, especially regarding employee experience surveys. Employees may hesitate to share information such as microaggressions, pay inequity, or favoritism because they fear being retaliated against by their supervisors or peers.
- Talent Acquisition and HR Business Partners: This pair can be so much more aligned than we typically see in companies. HRBPs can be a great sourcing tool for recruiters because they have a pulse on where skills are spread within the organization; instead, the two functions are often disjointed. HR executives should intentionally create touchpoints for them to work together.
- Learning and Development and Talent Acquisition: This pair struggles to smooth the transitions between the lifecycle phases. The biggest pain point in their relationship is a poor employee experience; poor workflows and handoffs require far too many DIY interventions from employees. This includes the transition from candidate to new hire and from experienced professional to a promotion or lateral transfer.

The People side of PCI marries the employee experience with solid HR systems and processes. The HR functional areas manage phases of the employee lifecycle, and they provide coverage and wisdom to the founder, C-suite, leaders, and employees. Founders are responsible for understanding who manages each employee lifecycle phase, and the founder along with the CHRO set the norms for leveraging the key factors to create a happier, more equitable employee experience within each phase.

Evolution to Equity

Lifecycle Phase	HR Functional Area Owner	Key Factor
Attraction	Talent Acquisition, HR Business Partners	Time
Selection	Talent Acquisition, HR Business Partners, Compensation and Benefits	Presence
Onboarding	Learning and Development, Talent Acquisition, HR Operations, Compensation and Benefits	Presence
Development	Learning and Development, Employee Relations and Compliance, HR Operations, Risk Management, HR Analytics	Money
Retention	HR Business Partners, HR Analytics, Talent Acquisition, Compensation and Benefits	Time
Separation	HR Business Partners, Employee Relations and Compliance, HR Operations, Risk Management	Attention

Chapter 14: Culture

In PCI, culture is not as abstract as we have been taught. On the contrary, cultures are intentionally designed by what founders do and what they allow to go unchallenged, both of which signal to employees what matters in the organization. Founders can be quite immature, myself included. We fly into business with high aspirations, surround ourselves with yes-men, then feel confused when we face scrutiny from outsiders or internal scandals.

There's a reason why companies seem dull as they mature. Structure, discipline, correction, and standards feel boring to us as founders because we champion disruption and eccentricity. The former tempers the flame of the latter before our obsession with disruption can destroy what we're building. This is the core of culture. Culture means bravely owning our strengths while correcting our weaknesses and neutralizing our threats. Cultures happen one decision, one employee, and one moment at a time.

We are never cultureless. I chuckle when founders tell me they want to "change the culture" in kickoff calls. I laugh even harder when they say they need employees to fit the culture rather than fight it. The reality is our culture changes whether we want it to or not. The organization's culture is a combination of the employer and consumer brand, communication norms, cross-functional synergy, and values alignment. These elements are always changing, even if just a little, and even if it means becoming more ingrained into the company's fabric. A true culture change process occurs through a discipline called organizational development.

Organizational Development

Organizational development (OD) is a set of planned activities intended to shift a company in one or more of four areas: structure, operations, employee capacity, or strategy.

- **Structure shift**: A change in the organization's hierarchy, reporting lines, or vertical split. Structural shifts can result from reducing the number of employees, hiring more employees, or reassigning employees to new roles.
- **Operations shift**: A change in the organization's core and/or cross-functional workflows. Operations shifts can result from simplifying current processes, adding complexity to current processes, automating processes, or outsourcing processes to improve efficiency and reduce expenses.
- **Employee capacity shift**: A change in the organization's core competencies, labor distribution, or required skill levels for survival within the organization. Employee capacity shifts can result from reskilling (assigning talent with transferable skills to new projects or teams), upskilling (training interested staff to perform new work), or reducing headcount or teams.
- **Strategy shift**: A change in the organization's goals, brand positioning, customer focus, or verticals. Strategy shifts can result from new market entrances or exits, consumer and/or employer brand refreshes, and shifts to the organization's structure, operations, or employee capacity.

Each shift has different goals, methodologies, and expected impacts. As we implement the shifts throughout the company, we'll watch our culture evolve into an equity-centered environment.

Structure

Structural OD interventions are how we commonly recognize the OD discipline. These interventions include reorganizations (moving departments to other areas of the company), reductions in force/layoffs, or mergers and acquisitions, which require integrating new team members into the existing company structure. This paints such a limiting picture of OD's impact. Organizational development goes further to impact structure by managing spans of control and segmenting verticals.

Managing Spans of Control

Managing spans of control is how we monitor reporting lines so people managers don't have too many or too few direct reports. When people managers have too many people to supervise, they lack the time to focus on coaching, which can lead to all types of inequity where they will naturally gravitate towards the "easy" employees who share their personality, educational background, or even race and gender. It can also increase the likelihood of them overcorrecting minor issues. Employees who could simply benefit from targeted development and coaching may end up being punished or ostracized because the supervisor is unable to find the time to customize a development plan.

A people manager can have too few direct reports as well. This is where cliques grow within the organization because the small team is so siloed that they adopt an "us versus them" mentality. It can be very difficult to integrate small teams into larger ones when they have been in their own world for years. I recall one client where two large organizations merged and a small HR operations team was completely blocking integration efforts. The large merger generated a lot of fear of layoffs, so most teams clamped down and refused to share access or information. This small HR operations team of three managed all of the global relocations and onboarding IT processes. Their refusal to work with other groups meant employee relocations and new hire onboarding were held in limbo week after week. It was a mess!

Having just the right amount of direct reports, what I called the Goldilocks Effect, means people managers have time to be an administrator and a coach, and they have time to perform their role's operational or strategic tasks. They also have time to focus on people manager development. People management is a skill, and it shouldn't just be a reward for longer tenure or a pacifier to retain talent. People need training to become great managers, just like they need training to become top performers.

Segmenting Verticals

Many founders segment verticals based on revenue potential or expense management. While this is important, vertical segmentation is primarily an opportunity to maximize talent's potential and accelerate fulfilling the company's long-term vision. Remember, as we manage the four Vs – verticals, viscosity, vision, and values – talent is our "how," not just the right products and services. We can significantly increase productivity when founders and the C-suite prioritize talent placement.

Vertical segmentation includes how we level employees and assign their job task groupings. Let's say 45% of our staff works in one of our three verticals. The way they are stacked within the vertical can create a promotional bottleneck where high performers cannot move up because they can't surpass their supervisor's level. Shifting high performers to a smaller vertical with a level upgrade can boost retention and job satisfaction. Job task groupings are the umbrellas for a role's job duties. They signal accountability, responsibility, and value-add. Instead of simply listing 10-20 job duties in a job description, consider grouping using 3-4 key areas. This can assist people managers in mobilizing talent to verticals where they can grow their skills or show them off for more recognition.

Operations

OD interventions boost operational efficiency and excellence. A technical definition of efficiency is the ratio of performance to work, which can be determined by asking how much energy we expend to be productive and minimize waste. This is a critical question in PCI because PCI's measurements include both tangible and intangible metrics. Operational efficiency can mean fewer leaves of absence and ease in information sharing. One is simple to count, but the other, not so much; though both are very important to project timelines, retention, and engagement.

On the other hand, operational excellence is a continuous improvement outcome, which can only be achieved when the organization's culture encourages and rewards the pursuit of "better." One result is beating the competition, but that's too simplistic when there are more meaningful outcomes such as a sense of belonging, fulfillment, and confidence. Efficiency and excellence are twins because they are the product of culture, and you'll likely birth one when you birth the other. Founders and C-suite teams can improve operational efficiency and excellence by prioritizing time-to-value and leveraging motivational guiding philosophies.

Prioritizing Time-to-Value

Time-to-value (TTV) is actually a marketing concept that measures how quickly a product or service benefits a customer. A longer TTV can frustrate customers and result in lower revenue and market interest. Similarly, if it takes "too long" for employees to believe there is mutual benefit in their role, they will either leave or disengage. I quoted "too long" because each employee has a different timeline. Studies have shown that by the end of one month in a role, employees know if they're headed for the door. Lowering the employee's TTV requires careful planning during onboarding, strategic checkpoints throughout their tenure, and competent managers who can spot at-risk employees and intervene appropriately. New hires or newly promoted employees should experience at least one win within the first 90 days. Even if the win is simply writing a report or connecting with a leader, this can be a powerful motivational tool.

TTV is an OD concern because its impact can spread throughout the organization, even if it begins as a problem on just one team, because no team operates exclusively in a silo. Slow timelines, blocks, stonewalled communication, and incompetence can become organizational cancers. OD tools and interventions can be lifesavers that improve the entire company's operations.

Motivating Through Philosophy

I'm a founder who loves a good slogan. I especially love alliteration – it's cheesy but memorable and easy to grab. One reason I love slogans is because they create a foundation for decision-making, conflict resolution, and synergy. Philosophies are simply grown-up slogans. Philosophies serve as guardrails to identify how low or how far we'll go as a company, as cheerleaders to encourage us to perform our best, and as a GPS to clue us into the aspirational next steps we'll take as an organization. At a minimum, founders should create a talent philosophy, compensation philosophy, and an organizational value model to keep the team motivated and focused.

The talent philosophy explains the company's value proposition to candidates and employees. It defines how you help them grow, how they should contribute to the overall vision, and what makes the company different from competitors. The compensation philosophy details the "why" for pay, bonuses, equity (if applicable), benefits and perks, recognition, and rewards. Money matters. Too much favoritism in the compensation structure can cause attrition to explode and foster resentment within teams. Finally, an organizational value model shares the guiding principles (see the Values section in Chapter 7). The philosophies help ground OD work in shared beliefs, which make change easier to accept and understand.

Employee Capacity

Founders create high-growth organizations. We may double and triple our headcount quickly to meet market demand, which means we will likely promote or move current staff as we scale. We need nimble employees who are capable of growing with us, but not every employee has the capacity to grow quickly enough. Employee capacity is the measure of productivity over a given period of time. We calculate capacity using inputs like competence in needed skill sets, change threshold and orientation, years of experience, organizational tenure, job interest, role clarity, and task clarity. These inputs create a complex web of risk and opportunity.

Growth is not easy to manage, but it's our responsibility to shepherd that growth, which is why it's so important to have great people managers. Each input carries a different weight for each employee. A new hire with only three years of experience but a passion for creating a new product can be just as valuable as the existing employee with 20 years of experience who was in the first group of company hires. The high job interest of the former plus the institutional knowledge of the latter can help the company be ready to go to market quickly without hiccups. The inverse is true as well. A veteran, moderately-disengaged employee who has bounced from team to team with no promotion can be just as dangerous to the company's viscosity as a new employee who lacks expertise in a critical skill.

OD interventions build capacity through workforce planning and talent management. Workforce planning uses a deductive approach to assess where there are staffing, leveling, or skills gaps that could undermine the organization's short and long-term goals. Leaders look for gaps, vacancies, and inefficiencies in the organizational chart and ecosystem. Workforce planning projects include succession planning, market research to assess talent availability and geographic spread, and strategic partnership alignment to attract more candidates to the hiring pool. Talent management is inductive and more personal. It looks at each team member's abilities, goals, and potential to align them with the right leader, work, and team. Talent management projects include training programs, performance management system improvements, and mentorship and/or sponsorship program development.

Strategy

OD interventions protect your organizational strategy from external influences including shifts in political leadership, emerging market trends, and global crises that can completely upend a business strategy. The ongoing Ukraine-Russia conflict and COVID-19 pandemic have shown how important resilience and agility are to a company's survival. OD supports founders in building agility and resilience by realigning success measures and balancing competing needs across the organization.

Realigning Success Measures

Founders live by measurement. How many more users bought premium accounts? How many engineers should we hire in Q3? How many impressions did we make on social media? How many new stores can we place our product in before the holiday rush? The numbers game is intense. OD is our tool for using the right calculations to get the right numbers at the right time. In particular, OD is critical for creating key performance indicators (KPIs) and identifying critical success factors (CSFs).

Balancing Competing Needs

OD is inherently cross-functional. Every functional area in the organization wants to minimize costs, boost productivity, and retain top performers. These aren't unique to one team; however, scarce resources and time constraints mean every team won't be the top priority at the same time. OD interventions take a birdseye approach to change management. They can see the connection points and risk factors that individual leaders may miss in their blind spots. OD is agnostic because the discipline focuses on the whole company rather than just an individual team.

OD is a discipline, so this chapter only scratches the surface of all of its models. Here's a quick resource to help you brainstorm where to start.

Model/Methodology	Area to Shift			
	Structure	Operations	Employee Capacity	Strategy
Action research model	●	●	●	●
Agile method		●	●	
Appreciative inquiry model	●	●	●	
Competing values framework		●	●	
Four frame model	●	●	●	●
Galbraith's star model	●	●	●	●
Kaizen method		●	●	
Kanban		●	●	
Lean methodology	●	●	●	
Lewin's 3-step model	●	●		●
McKinsey 7-S framework	●	●	●	●
Organization design	●		●	
Six Sigma methodology	●	●	●	
Tuckman's stages model		●	●	

OD practitioners are not cheap hires, so think carefully about how expansive your needs' reach is before assembling an OD team. Founders maximize OD intervention ROI through large-scale, cross-functional projects like launching a new HRIS system, merging the product and engineering teams under a single executive, or expanding the company's geographic footprint to a new office out-of-state. One workaround for applying OD methods to smaller needs could be to hire a Chief of Staff with strong OD skills and experience. The Chief of Staff role already acts in a cross-functional capacity.

Having them play double-duty for OD projects can save time and money because they are a teammate people already trust.

Another option is to bring on a consultant for targeted interventions. If you select this route, be clear on the "why." Consultants can be useful in four domains: building organizational, team, or leader readiness; designing or reconfiguring change projects; launching a project outside of the normal operational scope; or evaluating a project or change effectiveness. The founder or internal project owner should clarify the reason with the consultant before beginning an engagement. Consultants may not want to admit it, but few (if any) are great in all four domains. I'm certainly not, even though I have experience and competence in all four. My preferences are building readiness and designing projects because I'm most interested in the beginning of projects. When clients need someone to stick with them through all four domains, I either staff the last two with another consultant in my firm or pass on the project altogether. This saves the client and me time and heartache. Not all consultants will be this honest, so founders have to be willing to ask the right questions upfront.

Chapter 15: Inclusion

Inclusion is one aspect of a larger discipline known as diversity, equity, and inclusion (DEI). DEI work needs to run like any other work you may do in your company. It's not just about one-off communications and quick responses during a crisis. DEI work should have owners or people who are accountable for the work, who perform the work, and then clearly identify support roles that add value to the work. HR is not the only owner of DEI work nor is the HR team the only subject matter expert.

The DEI landscape has four main areas:

- **Community**: This is the oldest aspect of corporate DEI functions. It involves hiring, retention, promotions, employee experience management, training, and development. The community aspect of DEI is anything we do to increase and maintain representation and increase equity through sharing power and influence, including how we manage the employee lifecycle. It also includes philanthropy and how we engage with the geographic locations where our companies work.
- **Culture**: Likely the least understood aspect, DEI cultural norms mean equitable communication standards and practices, building an inclusive consumer and employer brand, and making sure the values of the company promote a sense of belonging. Culture is also building the organization's capacity for DEI change.
- **Product**: This is the go-to-market side of DEI, which includes the entire product or service landscape from research to conceptualization through product effectiveness and reach. It includes who the product is built for, how accessible it is, how scalable it is, and whether or not the product or service itself is biased.
- **Marketing**: This differs from culture because it looks at the development of consumer brands in how they are

implemented publicly for consumers. A consumer brand should be filtered through an equity lens. This means looking at the world in a way that does not seek to demean any specific groups to convince other groups to purchase it. This can be tricky when we think of luxury brands or items because they hinge on people having the perception of exclusivity and superiority, which is a socioeconomic bias and a microaggression in and of itself.

There are DEI initiatives within each of the four areas. If this list seems overwhelming, it should. DEI work is much more than we've acknowledged as founders. Eventually, all of these initiatives will likely be in action simultaneously, but for now, prioritize at least 1-2 in each area and scale accordingly. Sometimes the work overlaps, and sometimes it is distinct. The staffing of these initiatives is important because no DEI practitioner is an expert in every area.

Community	Culture
• Identity dimension-centered conference sponsorship • Employer brand development • Manager training programs • Employee development programs • Promotional pipeline development programs • Employee experience surveys • Employee resource groups (ERGs), affinity groups • Philanthropy and community outreach/engagement	• Employee relations functions • DEI communication teams • Employee development philosophy • Standards to embody and support company values • Culture audit process • Institutional knowledge archives • Formal corrective action • Lobbying standards and communications • Employee data dashboards
Product	**Marketing**
• Supplier diversity programs • Pricing ethics analysis • Accessibility gap analysis • Inclusive language for product descriptions • Ethical product development standards • Impact clauses for product launches and sunsets • Packaging accessibility analysis • Sustainability metrics including environmental impact analyses	• Inclusive product campaigns • Marketing channel diversification • Inclusive product and service focus groups • Marketing ethics development • Consumer brand development • Inclusive communications design • Accessibility guideline development • Consumer complaints process

Accountability & DEI Stakeholders

The Chief Diversity Officer (CDO) is one of the most easily recognized roles in DEI; however, there are so many more stakeholders involved in the work. They all have different tasks, levels of accountability, and levels of power and influence. One of the ways you can help to identify who does what in DEI is through a RASCI matrix, which is a fillable table used to assign roles and tasks in a project. There are a few variations for the RASCI matrix tool, but I prefer this one. RASCI stands for responsible, accountable, supporting, consulted, and informed.

- Responsible: The person assigned to complete the task.
- Accountable: The person who owns and/or makes final decisions for the task. This is usually a business leader.
- Supporting: The person who helps the "R" complete the task.
- Consulted: The person who provides information to complete the task.
- Informed: The person who receives information on milestones or completion of a task. This is usually a senior-level executive or their liaison.

R	A	S	C	I
Responsible	Accountable	Support	Consulted	Informed

Project Activity	Role 1	Role 2	Role 3	Role 4
Task 1	A	C	R	I
Task 2	A	S	R	C
Task 3	C	I	A	R
Task 4	C	R	S	A

Project managers regularly use RASCI matrices, but the tool is especially important in DEI because of the work's complexity. Appropriate role and task assignment allows leaders to see the distribution of work to avoid burnout, as well as how to receive updates when needed.

When we look at DEI initiatives by area, it's important to leverage the RASCI matrix to pick the best fit by skills and interest, not just by functional area. Just because something is a product inclusion initiative, it doesn't mean the product team should be responsible or even accountable. For example, HR team members may be responsible and accountable for attending a diverse hiring fair, while the product team might simply be the informed group because they wanted candidates for the hiring pool.

External DEI Impacts

External influences like investors, community and political leaders, competitors, and community partners impact your DEI journey in ways that can creep up secretly if you're not paying attention.

Political Leaders

This includes changes to local, state, and national laws as well as elections, which often put key issues at the forefront. Housing laws impact employees and your physical workspace locations, and employment and tax laws directly impact companies' bottom lines. Employees, brand fans, and customers may even request the company make public statements or lobby for certain causes. Founders must have a justification for why or why not we'll choose to speak out.

Outsourced Vendor Support

Most startups outsource many functions related to DEI when the company is small, so we lack critical internal monitoring systems and processes or teammates who can respond to issues proactively rather than managing crises. We never want to be caught off-guard or found scrambling when a moment requires a measured response. We can avoid these blunders by having eyes, skills, and resources watching and ready to respond appropriately.

Competitors

Competitors are another external influence because everyone is always trying to one-up each other. This is another danger in DEI because companies will always try to slightly outdo one another but never maximize their own journey. Although it can be exciting and rewarding to go tit for tat, it patronizes a marginalized group's pain to feel superior. This can backfire if the response to every injustice isn't equally as grandiose. If we invest in one marginalized group but have a muted response for another, that's going to upset people and could ruin the company's brands.

Investors

The investor community, in general, has been viewed negatively for their own issues and a lack of inclusion, so companies have to carefully vet their potential funding sources for their own inclusion journey and history. Companies should have very clear conversations about the expectations and parameters around their DEI journey before receiving funds. Founders should also research the investors' personal and professional histories. Remember, our ecosystem stakeholders' problems can easily become ours, so we need to know the risks upfront.

Building and then activating cross-functional DEI stakeholders internally helps us weather the inevitable changes that will occur as a result of all these external powers and influences.

Belonging – The Founder's Responsibility

DEI is constantly evolving. Power, privilege, and influence struggles sit at the root of evolution. In Part I, I shared how deeply ingrained systemic biases can be and how we all have biases that then intertwine with societal biases. In my own childhood, I escaped much of the daily overt racism other Blacks may have faced because I grew up in a predominantly Black city. The shock I experienced in my transition to undergrad at a predominantly white institution was really just me being introduced to the world everyone else already knew. These disruptions to our norms can feel disorienting. We have a responsibility, as founders, to help our teams navigate and cope with these disruptions and new norms. This is the heart of the concept known as belonging.

Belonging can be tricky because its meaning varies by the individual. The dictionary defines belonging as "to have the proper qualifications to be a member of the group" and "to be appropriately situated or placed." This fascinates me because we often think of belonging as our employees' responsibility. We tell them to self-advocate, find friends and allies, seek out mentorship, and learn office politics. But how do we facilitate this as founders? We may not or would rather pretend not to know the shadow and aspirational values and norms which make belonging difficult for employees on the margins. The truth is, belonging is the founder's responsibility. We must be aware of the sneaky, unspoken "qualifications," which can ostracize some of the team. We are required to situate team members in groups where they can thrive and avoid harm.

Bias has a way of spreading, like cancer, without much effort. This is why bias awareness is critical for founders, especially in recognizing their executive team's biases. Every hire, promotion, raise, reward, and partnership reflects a pattern. Ask yourself: Is the pattern worth repeating? How much space do I make for diversity across the identity dimensions? How often do I affirm differences? The answers are telling for where employees may feel most isolated.

Justice – A Reasonable Outcome

The term "justice" has gained traction in the last 5-10 years in DEI because of the need for reconciliation and recompense. While the intent of DEI is not a zero-sum game, its implementation has been zero-sum for many marginalized groups. Certain groups have overwhelmingly benefited from interventions like affirmative action (white women), mortgage subsidies and redlining (white veterans), contracting quotas (Hispanic/Latine, Asian, and Black men), and anti-harassment policies (cis-presenting gay and lesbian workers).

Hierarchies of injustice exist even within marginalized groups. Black Muslims are not embraced as openly as Black Christians, Filipino and Vietnamese professionals are not regarded as highly as Chinese and Japanese professionals, and larger bodies with apple-shaped or inverted-triangle-shaped bodies are not considered as marketable as those with pear-shaped or hourglass-shaped bodies. The ways humans discriminate against one another are endless.

We can't just apologize, walk away, and assume people will figure out how to improve their lived experiences. Just as injustice has been engineered and reinforced, justice requires consistent effort too. As a founder, consider what justice could mean for the organization across these three domains:

- **Geographic region**: Every nation, state, and local area has displaced marginalized groups based on race/ethnicity, socioeconomic status, or religion. It is important to understand the displacement patterns and impacts to not only avoid repeating them but to grow our awareness of how the patterns and impacts can shape our office's culture and synergy with the surrounding community.
- **Compensation equity**: Founders must have a deep understanding of all aspects of pay inequity. This includes unattributed and uncompensated labor, disparate corrective action for similar infractions, and unclear promotion standards.

It's not solely dollars; it's all the opportunities and pitfalls on the journey to the dollars.

- **Product and marketing impact**: Marginalized cultures are often the purveyors of "cool." There are a myriad of reasons why, such as perceptions of exoticism, the need to build countercultures for survival, and isolation from dominant group norms, to name just a few. We perpetuate harm when dominant groups co-op the cultural practices of other groups without permission, compensation, or acknowledgment.

Research extensively to find out who has been displaced or snubbed, why it happened, and how to reintegrate these groups back into the spaces where they undoubtedly had a major cultural (and likely economic) impact. It may take years to correct the wrongs, but the results are worth it. Fast fashion's reputation for low wages and poor working conditions, real estate's history of racial discrimination and redlining, and healthcare's differential treatment of poor and BIPOC people are a few examples of how these three domains can threaten your equity ecosystem and company. Keep in mind we may not have deliberately caused harm through our work; nevertheless, we are still players in a game that requires us to share responsibility for its future.

Chapter 16: Measuring PCI

By now, I've shared tons of ideas about what founders can accomplish in PCI. Your first thought is likely to find out what competitors and peers are doing, but that would be a mistake. Start with you, and stay there until you form a solid identity. Then, and only then, should you move to think outward.

One of the first things I do for my clients is summarize the survey data from my company's Equitable Culture and Design Assessment (ECDA), which you can find on my website. The client's first question is always, "How do we measure up against other people?" I have to tell them I don't do benchmarking for PCI because I don't know anybody who is doing it right. They are often shocked by that because they have staked their reputation on how much better or worse they do than another company. It feels almost blasphemous to hear criticism of the companies they idolize. If we measure ourselves against an imperfect ruler, we yield imperfect results because the reference measurement is off.

Benchmarking also doesn't affirm our own identity. Simply chasing after what somebody else does doesn't guarantee it's a fit for our own company, industry, or geographic location. What might be relevant for an entertainment company in New York City might be completely inappropriate for a consumer goods company in Idaho. A lot of startups live and die by data – we need a data point for everything. What we miss is how important the *quality* of that data is to measurement. Relevance is one of the highest factors in determining quality.

Measuring PCI impact and effectiveness is a combination of qualitative and quantitative analysis. It's deeper than just following trends or viral moments. Qualitative data may seem frivolous, but it's one of the easiest ways to contextualize quantitative data. Qualitative data is usually gathered with open-ended questions and responses.

It can give us insights into the feelings, vibes, and perceptions of the company, which can make a huge difference in the quantitative data. The qualitative insights give clues into what quantitative data to examine further. By combining qualitative and quantitative data, founders can align the company's equity ecosystem to the company's identity and avoid mission creep.

PCI Metrics

PCI initiatives have metrics just like every other function in our company. The simplest of these metrics are key performance indicators (KPIs) and critical success factors (CSFs). KPIs are output barometers while CSFs are input threats. KPIs and CSFs are neither explicitly quantitative nor qualitative – they can be either. In fact, it may be most useful to include quantitative and qualitative measurements for both.

KPIs are important because they indicate accelerants and bottlenecks within the company. KPIs could be more revenue, higher scores on experience surveys, or more positive feedback on social media. These wins aren't just boxes to check; they open the path for even more progress in PCI. They don't just measure numbers – they signal the potential multiplier effect of successful PCI interventions.

It's important to note KPIs are different from other performance indicators. A company can have over 20 performance indicators but likely only a few KPIs. A key performance indicator is distinct because it has a multiplier effect on the output and often has other dependencies attached. Founders set KPIs to spur greater motivation and make strides quickly. Achieving KPIs should get us to the next level in PCI faster.

On the other hand, CSFs are behaviors, attitudes, or people who could undermine our PCI work. They measure potential threats which can be mitigated with the right team, tools, and timing. CSFs can range from a lack of geographic presence to a history of microaggressions against a particular group. Most importantly, they represent inputs we should correct against rather than outputs we seek to bury. If we wait until the CSF has already hurt us, we are far too late.

CSFs can be difficult to identify at higher levels in the company because the founder and C-suite are so far removed from operational work. This is why employee feedback is critical. Their complaints and pain points are our radars for identifying what can halt our short and long-term progress. This is one of the areas where having the right C-suite in place matters most. If the C-suite suppresses what they consider negative feedback, then we won't understand the CSFs. We need bold truth-tellers who can sound alarms when needed, not pacifiers who baby us with platitudes.

Communication Flow

While KPIs and CSFs are very important measures, they hinge on our ability to communicate with stakeholders in our equity ecosystem. Communication flow is the number of organizational communication channels and the varying levels of intimacy and privacy within each. The communication channels should be robust enough to provide highly segmented data about stakeholder experiences. Communication is one of the most glaring measurements in PCI because it measures impact in both its presence and absence. A lack of communication may mean stakeholders don't feel comfortable issuing complaints or offering suggestions for improvement, and that's a problem. We should be very concerned because each person's identity includes over 50 dimensions, so there are thousands of opportunities to improve equity within the company.

Communications should be more than bulletins and crisis management announcements. It should be systemic. It's the content of what we say but also the pacing of sharing information, the approval process for who gets to share, and the appropriate weighting of the voices. Some examples of communication channels can be experience surveys and focus groups for each of the ecosystem stakeholders.

The way we measure the effectiveness of our communication channels is through the pace of response, the pressure of response, and the frequency of response.

- **Pace of response**: How quickly we respond. If a marginalized voice says something is wrong, and we take two years to respond, that is poor relationship management.
- **Pressure of response**: The intensity of the response, how far it resonates, and the publicity of the response. If a marginalized voice says something is wrong, and it takes 2 million more people to say it before we take action, we're mismanaging that relationship.
- **Frequency of response**: How often we are willing to address it and how far we are willing to go to address systemic problems. If somebody has to say something 25 times before we even start to investigate, we are mismanaging that relationship.

We have to create more channels and pipelines and develop a more complex communication system to make sure we hear our employees. I worked with a client recently, and I had to advise him that, as a leader, he is not hearing what's going on throughout the organization. Silence is actually a dog whistle that something is wrong. Founders and the C-suite shouldn't necessarily be embroiled in day-to-day gossip about what color shirt someone wore, but we do need to know any emerging patterns of dysfunction because that's how we prevent crises.

Integrated PCI

While I spent most of this section describing PCI as separate topics, they are interdependent and rarely occur as standalone activations. I'd be remiss to end the book without offering at least a few scenarios to illustrate how People, culture, and inclusion work intersect one another on your evolution journey. When applied intelligently, they make one another stronger. When applied recklessly, they further engineer inequity.

To understand why PCI is usually performed so recklessly, we first need to identify the culprits. Most organizations use in-house HR staff or HR vendors to perform operational People work, consultants for culture work through OD projects, and in-house but under-supported DEI staff or narrowly-focused DEI consultants for inclusion work. The HR staff is too overwhelmed with their day-to-day tasks to design and execute major change projects. Consultants typically operate from such an abstract, disconnected space that they lack the trust and integration to make the changes stick. The DEI staff is often iced out of important conversations on operational work and strategic business goals, so their work seems irrelevant and counterproductive to the company's current state. The result? Stagnation. Aggravation. Futility. Confusion.

There's a better way. First, founders should clarify the staffing needs for the PCI functions. While I raised caution earlier about bringing in consultants, they can be very helpful in establishing organizational readiness for PCI work. Organizational readiness is a body of work that includes creating strategy, designing team structures for the work, and/or coaching the C-suite to prepare them for the PCI team's needs. These are very important yet often overlooked activities. I've quit in-house roles at companies because of organizational chaos where I knew I'd never be able to get anything done until the C-suite gathered themselves. I love doing organizational readiness work as a consultant because I can use pointed language and be bold in my approach. Leaders aren't as open to in-house staff being blunt, and the in-house team may hold back because of fear of retaliation.

This brings me to my final point – admit your biases toward the PCI functions. We all have them. One common bias is assuming HR is there to protect the company at all costs. We aren't. Another is consultants must always have the right answers. We don't. Another is that DEI staff is primarily there to put out fires and pacify marginalized groups from complaining. We aren't. Locating our biases as founders is necessary to remove the silo walls between People, culture, and inclusion so we can solve issues at the root.

Conclusion: What's Next?

Evolution is a process. It requires tough choices, consistency, connection, and, yes, even some confrontation. Recognizing where we can improve is not for the weak; changing is for the strong. I trust you've experienced at least one "aha" moment while reading this book, and you are likely wondering what's next.

ACTION!

Evolution occurs through action, and our actions increase the power of momentum and the peace of self-sufficiency.

The Power of Momentum

Momentum supercharges our evolution towards equity. One of the reasons I love science disciplines is because they have an amazing ability to describe phenomena in a very calculated way. Momentum can be calculated using the formula "$p=m(v)$", or mass multiplied by velocity. In physics, the formula implies we do less work over time simply by staying in motion.

As a founder, our evolution to equity can be easily lost while scrambling to get the company off the ground, so it's important to understand the power of momentum. In equity evolution, momentum is what we are made of multiplied by how fast we're willing to go. If we take away some of our mass or slow people down because of a lack of synergy, we slow our entire organization down, making it nearly impossible to regain traction. Lost momentum leads to losing valuable resources, which are time and people. We can't get back the time it takes to get people to believe in us, our vision, and the product or service we offer. Reducing momentum could lead to missed waves of opportunity with our target customers or ideal candidates for employment.

When we lose what we could do at the moment, we lose out on more than just one opportunity – we miss many possibilities. And the power of possibilities is a founder's greatest asset. So whatever you do, keep moving forward and keep the momentum going.

The Peace of Self-Sufficiency

PCI proficiency hinges on self-sufficiency. One definition of self-sufficiency is confidence in your abilities and powers, which applies to PCI work. We may not always have the answers, but smart founders commit to building their confidence in PCI. We're confident in seeking to understand and mitigate our own biases. We're confident in growing an executive team that wants a healthy organization where our team feels a sense of belonging. We make the world better through our products and services. We're confident in our ability to iterate our PCI work over and over again. We're confident that even though the work of PCI is never done, we're resilient enough to stay the course, regardless of how many twists and turns it has.

That should bring us peace. Peace is not the absence of turbulence but rather the confidence that we have the tools and skills to navigate through it. Self-sufficiency reflects how people enjoy our company for the value we bring to them and the world. Some of the most beloved and well-respected brands in PCI work have been able to tap into their own unique version of what PCI means for them, even through turbulence and mistakes. This is important because it makes the work sustainable. What makes people fall in love with us? Own that. Keep being that. Grow that.

I will tell you the same thing I tell my PCI coaching clients: I am so proud of you. You've taken an important first step in evolving on your equity journey by reading this book. Now, the work continues. The information contained in these pages is meaningless if you do not take action on it. If it feels overwhelming, take a step back and decide where to start. What aspects of PCI work would be most beneficial in your business right now? Make a list and then create a plan to work through it. Involve your frontline and executive teams in the strategy and let them contribute to executing on the plan. At the end of the day, while this work is the sole responsibility of the founder, it will take a village to get it right and make it sustainable.

I look forward to meeting who you and your amazing company will become after embarking on this most rewarding journey.

Dimensions of Identity Tables

Core Schema	
Dimension	Definition
Disability Status	Whether or not you have an identified physical or health-related impairment.
Ethnicity	The state of belonging to a group that shares common national or cultural traditions.
Gender	One's sex, selected identlty, or behavioral expression of one's sex.
Generation	Age group based on when you were born.
Race	A grouping based on shared physical and/or social qualities.
Sexual Orientation	Romantic and/or sexual attraction to the same, opposite, or no gender.

Secondary Schema	
Dimension	Definition
Caregiver Status	Whether or not you are taking care of a loved one, be it a child or adult.
Childhood Primary Language	The language most frequently and most fluently spoken to you by your caregivers.
Education Level	Your highest level of completion towards a degree, certification, or license.
Family Size	The number of people in what would be considered your nuclear family, including yourself.
Geographic Location	The place or places where you currently reside.
Primary Language	The language(s) you speak most frequently and most fluently.
Relationship Status	Whether or not you are currently partnered or in a committed relationship.
Religion/Spirituality	Your current belief system, regardless of whether or not it aligns to a specific group or denomination.
Socioeconomic Status (SES)	Your income and/or level of wealth.

Family Schema	
Dimension	Definition
Accent	The natural or elected tone based on where you live.
Birth Order	Your position in the sequence of children in your nuclear family.
Birthplace	The city or region of your birth
Childhood Religion/Spirituality	The religious or spiritual beliefs of your primary caregivers, especially if you were forced to participate in those religious activities.
Childhood SES	The socioeconomic status of your primary caregivers
Country of Origin	The nation in which you were born
Dialect	The colloquial language or slang used by a particular group of people, which can be dependent upon race, ethnicity, economic status, sexual orientation, etc.
Family Political Leanings	The general political party or leanings of your nuclear family.

Work Schema	
Dimension	Definition
Industry	The sector in which you primarily work or have the most experience in
Military Affiliation	Whether or not you belong to a branch of the military, and if so, which branch.
Occupation	The name of the work you do (example: doctor, lawyer, custodian).
Seniority/Tenure	How long you've been working in an industry or for a company.
Title Level	Your job title group (example: director, manager, coordinator).
Union Affiliation	Whether or not you belong to an organized labor group.
View of Authority	Your perspective on people who have authority over you. Some people view authority as absolute or a partner, while others view it as something to be defeated or lack respect for it.

Intrapersonal Schema	
Dimension	Definition
Attachment Style	How you form bonds with other people and the quality of those bonds. There are four attachment styles: • Secure • Insecure: Anxious • Insecure: Avoidant • Insecure: Disorganized
Cognition/Learning Style	The way in which you retain information best. There are three learning styles: • Visual • Auditory • Kinesthetic
Conflict Resolution Style	Your response to a conflict situation. Thomas Kilmann's five conflict resolution styles are: • Collaborating • Competing • Avoiding • Accommodating • Compromising
Intelligence	Visual-spatial, musical, bodily-kinesthetic, interpersonal, verbal-linguistic, logical-mathematical, naturalistic, and intrapersonal.
Mental Health Diagnosis	Whether or not you have a diagnosed mental health disorder.

Nonverbal Communication Style	The way you use parts of your body (other than your voice) to communicate. This includes facial expressions, gestures, para linguistics (loudness or tone), body language, proxemics (personal space), gaze, haptics (touch), and artifacts (accessories on your body like tattoos or jewelry. Many of these communication styles are cultural as well.
Personality Type	The dominant characteristics of who you are. These can be assessed differently through a variety of different tests, but it is dependent on how comfortable you are choosing how to define yourself.

Sociocultural Schema	
Dimension	Definition
Alcohol Consumption	The frequency and quantity of drinking alcoholic beverages.
Fraternal Affiliation	Belonging to a fraternity or sorority group.
Hobbies	Recreational and/or social activities.
Nicotine Usage	The frequency and quantity of using any nicotine or tobacco products.
Political Ideologies	Identifying with the beliefs of an established political party.
Political Party Affiliation	Belonging to or identifying with an established political party.
Social Causes	The belief in or support of various efforts to shift societies.
Substance Abuse History	Whether or not you've been diagnosed as a substance abuser or addict.
Substance Usage	The use of any mind-altering substances for recreational or medical use.
Trauma History	History of singular or patterned adverse experiences, particularly those related to Adverse Child Experiences (ACEs).

Appearance Schema	
Dimension	Definition
Body Markings	Any natural or forced alterations to the skin including tattoos, tribal markers, moles, skin tags, scars, etc.
Body Shape	The shape or figure of your body based on the distribution of your muscle and fat.
Eye Color	The tone of your iris and sclera (the whites of your eyes).
Hair Color	The tone and shade of your hair, including any highlights.
Hair Type	Whether your hair is straight, wavy, curly, or kinky, as defined by the Hair Type Chart using 1-4 and A-C.
Height	How tall you are and the perception of your height group.
Skin Tone	The tone and undertones of your skin. Tones include, light, fair, medium, and dark (deep). Undertones include warm, cool, and neutral.
Style of Dress	Your preferred style of dress.
Voice Pitch	The perceived frequency of your voice.
Voice Tone	The perceived quality of your voice.
Weight Category	The classification of weight status based on your Body Mass Index. This includes underweight, healthy weight, overweight, obese, and severely obese.

About the Author

Kalyn Romaine is an organizational psychologist, executive coach, and former corporate executive who has been successfully leading People, culture, and inclusion transformation for over 15 years at unicorn startups, Fortune 100 companies, nonprofits, and the nation's largest city governments. Her expertise has transformed organizations such as Amazon, The Walt Disney Company, Verizon, and Zapier, among others.

Born and raised in the predominantly Black metropolis of Detroit, Kalyn fully embraces her equity evolution, which includes recognizing deeply held biases and accepting a penchant for being far too outspoken to the powers that be. She is a proud alumna of the University of Michigan at Ann Arbor, DePaul University, and Adler University. Her largely homogenous collegiate and graduate school experiences triggered a reflection on the negative impact of bias toward marginalized groups and systemic inequity from which her career in People, culture, and inclusion was born.

Kalyn is completing her Ph.D. at Adler University in Industrial and Organizational Psychology, and her dissertation research explores how to optimize Black men's employee experience. Her studies include degrees in organizational psychology, sociology, and management, as well as certifications in Lean Six Sigma Black Belt, HR, change management, and professional coaching.

As the founder of Dream Forward Consulting, she leverages her years of deep experience and learning to support leaders in launching and scaling People, Culture, and Inclusion (PCI) work within their organizations. This global work has taken her to places like New York City, Los Angeles, Accra, Ghana, and Durban, South Africa. Now based in Atlanta, Kalyn is proud to continue her work as a champion for all people regardless of race, sexual orientation, socioeconomic background, religious or political beliefs, and any other dimensions of identity. Learn more about her at www.kalynromaine.com.

Made in the USA
Middletown, DE
04 April 2024